IDEA WORK

IDEA WORK
LESSONS OF THE EXTRAORDINARY
IN EVERYDAY CREATIVITY

ARNE CARLSEN

STEWART CLEGG

REIDAR GJERSVIK

CAPPELEN DAMM
AKADEMISK

© CAPPELEN DAMM AS, 2012

ISBN 978-82-02-40337-9

1. edition, 2.corrected printing 2013

Cover design: Snøhetta Design
Cover photo: Snøhetta Design
Typesetting: Snøhetta Design/ Kind Design
Printing and binding: Livonia Print SIA, Latvia

www.cda.no
e-mail: akademisk@cappelendamm.no

WHAT? ANOTHER BOOK ON CREATIVITY AND INNOVATION?! WELL, NO. AND YES.

Idea Work is a book about the collective practices of organizations that live from their ideas. These are powerful ideas: the book tells how a global oil company produces ideas about where to drill in order to find new oil fields; it explores how an international architecture firm manages its idea processes from the first sketches to the finished building and beyond; it investigates how business lawyers transform deep legal knowledge and experience to fit contexts and situations that are just a little different from any case they have faced before; it describes business and systems development processes as complex, collective activities that combine solid knowledge with imaginings of new demand.

These are all stories about creativity and innovation. So yes, this is a book about all these things, but seen in a new light rather than through the old established windows of unique individual attributes and proclivities. This is not a book about creativity that celebrates individuals, describes techniques and tells stories taken from the marketing industry. Nor is this a book that reduces innovation to a set of processes with decision gates controlled by advanced, copyrighted project management systems. The book describes Idea Work as collective practices that can be found in many organizations, even in organizations that we do not normally think of as creative. While these practices produce extraordinary results in many cases, they are interwoven in the fabric of everyday work. Our intention is not to downplay the role of important individuals, but we place emphasis on how organizations are able to create contexts in which they can flourish and how collective effort is required to move from brilliant ideas to final results.

The *Idea Work* project, upon which this book is based, was a large-scale, empirical research project co-sponsored by the Norwegian Research Council under the "User-driven research based innovation"-program (BIA), and led by a group of researchers at SINTEF. In this project we worked with six organizations, all of which have been leaders in their respective industries. We have tried to make sense of the various practices for working with ideas in the six organizations, asking: how do people in these organizations generate, mould, communicate and realize ideas when at their best? What we found is that there are many patterns of work that are very similar and commonly shared across quite different industries and organizations. This book is about those patterns. We call them qualities of extraordinary idea work.

The Idea Work book is one of the products of the larger project and, as is the case with all other knowledge products, it is the result of a set of collective processes and practices created by a group of knowledgeable and creative individuals. We would especially like to mention the following persons: Tord Mortensen initiated the first idea work project with the explorers at Statoil, has been a key contributor throughout the process and is co-author of four of the chapters in the book. Grete Håkonsen was central in initiating the project, was lead researcher in one of the partner organizations and coined the phrase "Idea Work". Aina Landsverk Hagen, Gudrun Skjælåen Rudningen and Arne Lindseth Bygdås have been part of the core project team throughout the project period, as researchers in one or more of the companies, and as contributors of interviews, observations – including graphical and video material – as well as in discussions. They are also co-authors on chapters in the book. Maria Lundberg, Kjersti Bjørkeng, Bjørn Haugstad and Åsne Lund Godbolt have also made important contributions in the project bothin the work with participating organizations and in discussions. We, the project group including the authors, feel a collective ownership to the ideas and concepts of Idea Work.

Persons in the companies that we write about in this book have had a profound influence on the ideas that we communicate. They were passionately interested in learning about and improving their own practices, and so they gave us, the researchers, free access to their inner workings. We interviewed managers, employees, partners and customers; we have been members of teams and observers of teams, and we have run processes in which managers, employees and researchers have sat down to reflect on results and new concepts so that they could feed the ideas back into the companies' practices. We have used approaches from ethnography, action research and participant observation and have often been deeply immersed in the life world and practices of the organizations we researched. We appreciate the engagement of the managers and owners who had the courage to learn from research, and the employees who had the curiosity, time and inclination to take part in the creation of new knowledge. There are many individuals in these organizations who have made an extra effort to bring the Idea Work project forward. We would especially like to mention Pål Haremo, Morten Rye-Larsen, Trond Lien and John Reidar Granli in Statoil; Ole Gustavsen, Marianne Sætre, Jenny Osuldsen and Frank Kristiansen in Snøhetta; Carl O. Geving, Kai Thøgersen and Stig Berge in Thommessen; Atle Christiansen, Per-Otto Wold and Magnus Køber at Thomson Reuters Point Carbon; Anne-Marte Kjersem, Tina Steinsvik Sund, Roger Teimansen, Eivind Winther and Trine Folkow in SpareBank 1 Alliance, as well as Kjersti Løken Stavrum, Kjetil Østli and Kristin Stoltenberg at *A-magasinet*.

We also owe gratitude to people at Snøhetta Design who has put shape, color and flair to the book. They are Joao Doria, Kristian Allen Larsen, Ole Gustavsen and Anine Anderson. Thank you.

The academic advisors of the Idea Work project are internationally renowned academics who contributed their knowledge, intellectual skills and time to interact with the project in many different ways. Throughout the project, the group has included Professor Elena Antonacopoulou (University of Liverpool Management School, UK), Professor Jane Dutton (Center for Positive Organizational Scholarship, Stephen M. Ross School of Business, University of Michigan), Associate Professor Roger Klev (Department of Industrial Economics and Technology Management at the Norwegian University of Science and Technology), Associate Professor Tyrone Pitsis (Newcastle University Business School), Professor Karl Halvor Teigen (Department of Psychology, University of Oslo) and co-author of this book, Professor Stewart Clegg (CMOS Centre for Management and Organisation Studies, University of Technology Sydney). We have organized symposia and sub tracks with one or more of these collaborators at four different international conferences. A particularly valuable part of this collaboration has been, in close cooperation with Jane Dutton, the compiling and editing of a book of 40 stories about generative moments in qualitative research. Research is indeed also idea work, and many of the patterns of being extraordinary that we write about here have their parallels in the world of research. We invite you to have a look at this work; it is Carlsen, A. and Dutton, J. E (eds.). 2011. Research Alive: *Exploring Generative Moments in Doing Qualitative Research. Copenhagen: Copenhagen Business School Press.*

Much of what we write about wonder and the aesthetic and embodied nature of idea work is inspired by the collaboration with a person with particularly deep knowledge about those parts of life: Professor Lance Sandelands (also at the Stephen M. Ross School of Business, University of Michigan). We are grateful for those sparks of insight and inspiration.

Our initial work on the present book has been sponsored by grant number 187952/I40 of the Norwegian Research Council, where Lise Våland Sund has been a valuable collaborator. We are also grateful to Tor Paulson of Cappelen Damm who showed much enthusiasm and initiative in bringing this project to the finish line.

Writing books, of course, is nothing but idea work. As such, it is a deeply collective endeavor both in the activities being performed and the many sources, stories and voices drawn upon. So in extending a heartfelt thank you to all our partners and collaborators, we can only hope that the ideas presented will leave our shared cradle and thrive in the minds, ambitions, hopes, language and practice of our readers.

Oslo, 15.11.12, Arne Carlsen, Stewart R. Clegg and Reidar Gjersvik

IDEA WORK IS

INTERWOVEN

AFFECTIVE

MATERIAL

CONTROVERSIAL

PREPPING

The practice of carefully preparing, building, and revitalizing knowledge so as to maximize its potential for effective use in the moment of creation.

ZOOMING OUT

Stepping back from immersion in data and analysis of ideas of particulars and moving to big-picture thinking, letting go of details, and seeking the simplifying core.

CRAVING WONDER

The sensuous experience of being in a mystery, a combination of feeling startled and engaging in passionate search. Wonder underpins all imagination, empathy, and deep interest in anything beyond self.

ACTIVATING DRAMA

Calling people to adventure –into Battles, Mysteries, Missions, Cathedral building, Treasure Hunts or the needs of the human Other – in ways that recruit their utmost capabilities and desires, asking: "Why do we come to work here? What is really at stake?"

DARING TO IMAGINE

Boldly venturing forth into unknown territory through creating shared imaginings, cultivating a language of possibility, handling failure, and providing encouragemen

GETTING PHYSICAL

Moving from over-dependence on electronic media towards *materializing* and *visualizing* ideas in artifacts; *touching* ideas, *sketching* ideas, *gesticulating* around ideas, and *moving* while doing idea work.

DOUBLE RAPID PROTOTYPING

A work form that seeks to force speedy production, testing and improvement of half-worked ideas so that they are shared and bolstered at an early stage of development.

LIBERATING LAUGHTER

Processes of energizing co-creation through playfulness, puns, and humor aimed at building social ties, reducing seriousness, relaxing constraints in thinking, and encouraging original combinations of knowledge.

GENERATIVE RESISTANCE

Acknowledging doubt, friction, and criticism, not as noise to be avoided, but as levers with which to question the given and enhance imagination in everyday work.

PUNK PRODUCTION

Using audacity and direct, self-initiated action to mobilize agai established ways, opening up ar realizing ideas with high levels c originality and value.

INTERWOVEN

AFFECTIVE

MATERIAL

CONTROVERSIAL

WHY TALK ABOUT IDEA WORK, AND WHAT DOES IT MATTER?

ARNE CARLSEN, STEWART CLEGG AND REIDAR GJERSVIK

What does it take to find oil in an area where many have tried but failed? What does it take to design buildings that become award-winning, culturally symbolic landmarks? What might the best architects, oil explorers, lawyers, investigative journalists, and business developers in banking and trading analytics have in common? The answer is that they work in surprisingly similar ways when they work with ideas.

This is a book about "idea work": Activities concerned with generating, selecting, realizing, nurturing, sharing, materializing, pitching, and communicating ideas in organizations. For most organizations, idea work is simply the main basis for creating value, whether it is in everyday project work and interaction with clients or development of new products and services.

We are not interested in just any kind of idea work; our focus is on the exemplary, on those ideas that are capable of powering breakthroughs. We present the key features of extraordinary idea work. These features have been identified through a four-year research project in organizations which have demonstrated leading capabilities in their industries over time: an architectural firm, the exploration units of a major oil company, a law firm, an alliance of savings banks, a supplier of trading analytics, and a weekend magazine. These organizations share in common that much of what they do and the very basis for their competitive advantage, is tied to work on ideas: for example, ideas of where to find oil, ideas of architectural concepts, feature articles, or new cash payment systems.

The six organizations also have in common distinct qualities of idea work when at its best, despite representing widely different industries. We will present ten such qualities here. Together, these ten qualities make up a language for idea work in organizations, a language of high academic originality and practical relevance.

Academically, the concept of idea work responds to a recent stream of research that has an explicit focus on how creativity is inherent in everyday work (e.g., Murphy 2005, Hargadon and Bechky 2006, Sawyer and DeZutter 2009) and moves away from a previous research focus on individuals or laboratory settings (Sternberg and Lubart 1999, Kurtzberg and Amabile 2001). What people actually do when being creative and working with ideas tends to disappear into averages, statistics, and assumed co-variations of variables. We know far too little about the concrete processes of collective creativity. The ten qualities of idea work presented in the book make up empirically grounded descriptions of precisely such processes – descriptions that we hope will inspire further comparative and process-oriented research.

Practically, we set out to create a research-based, tested, and usable language for a kind of work that dominates many organizations but has so far received modest attention. Idea work includes but is not limited to what we normally think of as creativity. It involves not only moments of creative breakthrough but also all the major and minor activities that lead up to breakthroughs and follow from them, such as preparation and analysis, peer assistance and critique, or repeated interactions and experiments among users. With the ten described qualities of extraordinary idea work at hand, we hope people across many sectors of the economy will be inspired to try out new ways of interacting and collaborating, whether they are line managers, project managers, specialists, front line workers, or people involved in any development activity.

This is a book about practice and how we talk about practice. Idea work is simply all the things that people do together when working with ideas. Our way of getting close to practice has not been to minutely analyze isolated episodes of group interactions or to spend years in ethnographic immersion after which we, as independent researchers, then emerge to convey definitive "answers" to our research questions. Rather, while also involving such methods, our approach has been one of repeatedly involving practitioners in our analysis and of testing out preliminary findings in real work settings. We have sought to do research *with* practitioners, not *on* them. Trying to make our learning co-generative, we have thus continually posed questions such as: "Here are what we currently perceive as the qualities of idea work at its best in your organization. How does this representation look to you? Which of these qualities seem more/less important, more/less well described? How does this compare to what we saw in organization X? How can these insights be acted upon when working with concrete challenges ahead? What, then, can be learned?"

We shall say more about our research approach – but first: What did we find? What does extraordinary idea work look like?

QUALITIES OF
EXTRAORDINARY IDEA WORK

Let us start with a story. Asked about how the main idea behind the new Opera building in Oslo, Norway, was generated, Kjetil Trædal Thorsen, founder and senior partner at Snøhetta, answers with the following:

> "Much of it is about being reluctant in starting the design and not trying to design a building. We have these very long conversations. There are an incredible amount of contextual conditions that we have to talk through, again and again, ranging from function to environmental issues to the constellation of objects that are needed to materials to the situation of the building and the wider landscape. We try to integrate all these elements. There are these circles of conversation, a joint walk in references. And the purpose is to generate similar images in everyone's head before we start to draw. Architecture is about generating these joint imaginings of what could be... It is not necessary that all the people involved have the same imaginations all the time, but the basic elements of the concept need to be shared by all the people driving the projects... We also invite a larger group of people who do not work here into these conversations, for example a composer, a libretto writer, or a ballet director. Nobody decides the agenda for such a meeting. We just start talking freely about the opera, what opera is, what story-telling is, inside the building or in terms of how the actors meet the audience and vice versa."

Thorsen's account of the work behind the Norwegian Opera building may sound particular to architectural work and relevant only for that world. It is not. The long conversations at Snøhetta have many qualities that are strikingly and surprisingly similar to what oil explorers do when they come up with ideas of where there is oil to be found, or what lawyers do when they arrive at ideas for how they might win major litigation cases. Basic to all three is *prepping*. Oil explorers prep when they systematically collect and analyze seismic data, well logs, and regional data. Lawyers prep when establishing the juridical facts of a case and reviewing previous cases. All of them prep by systematically providing a group of people with the knowledge that may generate new ideas and alternative ways of combining them: alternative case strategies, alternative conceptions for a building, or alternative prospects for where oil can be found. And all use various types of outsiders in the process – whether clients, end users, or colleagues from distant court areas or other exploration regions. Prepping involves the practice of carefully preparing and revitalizing knowledge in a way that maximizes its potential for effective use in the moment of creation. Without such preparation, great ideas will never emerge. Again, in the words of Kjetil Trædal Thorsen:

> "There may be collective aha! experiences but this never happens independently of an analysis that precedes it. Knowledge is the very basis for all. It is simply unthinkable to pull aha-moments out of thin air. You need basic knowledge about the place, about the project, about the program."

Prepping is one of ten qualities of extraordinary idea work that we present in this book: ten sets of practices by which high-value ideas are generated and realized in organizations.

Another quality of extraordinary idea work, one that underpins the long conversations of prepping, is *wonder*. Individuals who excel in idea work have in common a capacity to experience feelings of wonder in their work and to invoke wonder in others. These individuals notice things others might pass over. They see peculiarities in the normal. They dwell on the strange. They tolerate being in a state of not knowing. Wonder is the sensuous experience of being in a mystery, a combination of feeling startled and being engaged in a passionate search. It is in wonder that people stay and dwell in their long conversations, become engaged with the full repertoire of what they know, and immerse themselves in the search.

A third quality of extraordinary idea work is *generative resistance*. Great ideas are not born in blissful harmony. Ideas need to be confronted with criticism before they become great and are often born in adversity. According to Senior Architect Marianne Sætre of Snøhetta, tough problems are the main source of energy and creativity in any project. For Exploration Manager Thomas Reed, of Statoil, the hardest thing to do is to convince young people that there is still oil to be found in areas where many others

"And very early in the process, this thing about thresholds emerged, a sequence of thresholds, like the story of the movement to and into the Opera building and outside again. The type of adventure this is supposed to be comes before you think about form. The notion of thresholds also means moving from room to room and from situation to situation. None of us imagined what it might look like at this stage. But everyone agreed that there is something important in the idea of thresholds that we should explore further."

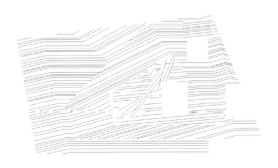

have already searched. And as Thor Ragnar Klevstuen, of SpareBank 1, says, confronting the tough challenges of handling cash payment for social clients was the generative source behind a whole portfolio of cash management services. Ideas flourish where resistance and problems are not avoided but rather confronted and made generative.

We have devoted a separate chapter of the book to each of the ten qualities of extraordinary idea work. A summary of the qualities is presented in Table 1 next page. As shown in the table of contents and associated pages, pp 10-13, these ten qualities can be grouped in four overall categories that have also determined the layout of the book: that idea work is interwoven, affective, material and controversial.[1]

Each of the ten chapters starts with one or more stories that exemplify what this particular quality of idea work looks like. We take the reader backstage in six organizations that all have proven capabilities of idea work and describe ways of working that are surprisingly similar across the different industries these organizations operate within. The ten qualities of extraordinary idea work have (with some exceptions, such as "double rapid prototyping") not been previously described in literature on innovation and creativity at work. Thus, we believe these are ways of working that will provide readers with terms and examples that may help them to understand their own work experiences and can serve as an inspiration for improving their practices.

TABLE 1 TEN QUALITIES OF EXTRAORDINARY IDEA WORK

NAME OF QUALITY	DEFINITION
Prepping	The practice of carefully preparing, building, and revitalizing knowledge so as to maximize its potential for effective use in the moment of creation.
Zooming out	Stepping back from immersion in data and analysis of ideas of particulars and moving to big-picture thinking, letting go of details, and seeking the simplifying core.
Craving wonder	The sensuous experience of being in a mystery, a combination of feeling startled and engaging in passionate search. Wonder underpins all imagination, empathy, and deep interest in anything beyond self.
Activating drama	Calling people to adventure – into Battles, Mysteries, Missions, Cathedral building, Treasure Hunts or the needs of the human Other – in ways that recruit their utmost capabilities and desires, asking: "Why do we come to work here? What is really at stake?"
Daring to imagine	Boldly venturing forth into unknown territory through creating shared imaginings, cultivating a language of possibility, handling failure, and providing encouragement.

NAME OF QUALITY	DEFINITION
Getting physical	Moving from over-dependence on electronic media towards *materializing* and *visualizing* ideas in artifacts, *touching* ideas, *sketching* ideas, *gesticulating* around ideas, and *moving* while doing idea work.
Double rapid prototyping	A work form that seeks to force speedy production, testing, and improvement of half-worked ideas so that they are shared and bolstered at an early stage of development.
Liberating laughter	Processes of energizing co-creation through playfulness, puns, and humor aimed at building social ties, reducing seriousness, relaxing constraints in thinking, and encouraging original combinations of knowledge.
Generative resistance	Acknowledging doubt, friction, and criticism, not as noise to be avoided, but as levers with which to question the given and enhance imagination in everyday work.
Punk production	Using audacity and direct, self-initiated action to mobilize against established ways, opening up and realizing ideas with high levels of originality and value.

We write of "qualities", and the use of this term is particularly deliberate on our part. We do not describe ten distinctly different work practices or methods that one can readily implement. Instead, we are talking about qualities as different aspects and patterns of the same practice. The qualities are not mutually exclusive but complementary; indeed, they are often interwoven, so that a typical story of people doing concrete idea work will often allude to several qualities at the same time.

These qualities are not singular skills: good idea work is not about doing only one thing right. Rather, it requires mastering many skills, of which some are contradictory. For example, systematic prepping and dwelling in wonder are very different qualities from rapid bursts of prototyping and zooming out; generative resistance entails very different qualities from building belief, and the intense engagement in activating drama can differ greatly from the ironic distance of liberating laughter. Idea work may mean seeking undisturbed attention, allowing the mind to soar in a way that gives free rein to imagination. It involves selectivity as well as maintaining openness; it requires passion against moments of existential pain and anguish, and calls for experience to be held up against fresh views. Truly striving for creativity entails the ability to exercise such contradictory qualities in one's practice. Related observations have been made in research on creative individuals: they tend to inhabit contrasting personality traits (Csikszentmihalyi 1996: pp. 51–76), but the actual collective practices that sustain these individuals, our focus, remains under-explored.

WHY CALL IT IDEA WORK?

The concept "idea work" provides a language of practice for talking about how professionals promote creativity in organizations (Coldevin et al. 2012). It is a language that recognizes creativity as interwoven in daily work and as something people do together. Creativity in organizations is usually defined in terms of processes that produce outcomes that are both novel and useful (Amabile 1996). It is not enough that an outcome is considered original. Only those variations of new and existing processes, products, and services that key stakeholders consider valuable are truly creative (Csikszentmihalyi 1999). Much creativity research is grounded in psychology, and, as a research field, it has had a predominant focus on individuals (Sternberg and Lubart 1999). Much of the common sense knowledge about what it means to be creative is mired in myths. There are myths about creativity as something stemming from the use of general techniques or something that takes place on away-days, and in big leaps. And there are myths of the heroic and ingenious individual (typically male) struggling in loneliness before achieving some breakthrough.

Andrew Hargadon (2003: pp. 3–32) has convincingly debunked the mythical portrayal of Thomas Edison as a singular genius inventor. The name "Edison" became associated with the achievements of the social practice of the Menlo Park Laboratory where some 15 "muckers", as the engineers called themselves, managed to combine known technologies in new ways – thus bridging small worlds and creating new ones. Edison, for all practical purposes, is more correctly the name source of a certain place and practice rather than a lone achiever. It signifies a commercialization of a collective effort and practice under a branded entrepreneurial label.

Focusing on the individual and on breakthroughs alone would be as misleading as trying to understand the success of Barcelona, the soccer club, by looking only at the star player, Lionel Messi, and at the moments when goals are scored. Many consider Messi to be the best soccer player the world has ever known. He has won numerous individual awards (for example, the Golden Ball Award in 2009, 2010, and 2011) and trophies (Champion League, 2010 and 2011). It is equally recognized that so far Messi has performed well below his top potential when playing for Argentina's national team. So, while not forgetting the importance of individuals, the point here is that star soccer players and idea work stars are always part of a larger social practice.

Ideas are not just concepts or mental impressions. Ideas are a fundamental ontological category of being – ways of being in the world. Idea work as a concept is inspired by the classical pragmatist tradition of William James, Charles Sanders Peirce, and John Dewey, where creativity is situated in the everyday. For Peirce (1878/1958), clear ideas require considerable work to be such that, when apprehended, they can be recognized wherever they are met and can be seen as unique. Idea work "works" successfully when the application of its product makes a significant difference in our evaluation of a proposed solution to a problem at hand, whether in philosophy or in our everyday life.

FOR THE LOVE OF IDEAS

When asked what engages him most in his work and what makes him truly come alive in his profession, senior explorer and professor in geology, Harry Doust answers with the following:

> "What gets you up in the morning – that sort of feeling? I think it is the thrill of exploration, of exploring something new, of overcoming uncertainty, a curiosity about how the natural world works. It is trying to explain something, knowing that you'll never have all the information that you need. We deal with so much uncertainty in exploration that I think none of us has huge expectations that we are going to be more than partially correct at best, but living with uncertainty allows your mind to soar, to fly with the birds. It allows you an amazing range of freedom of thinking."

Harry's answer illustrates that several of the key qualities of extraordinary idea work speak to aspects that go beyond the making of new products and services, beyond striving for competitive advantage. In a very profound sense, people come alive when they work with ideas. The quality of "craving wonder" tells us how people gain passionate interest in ideas, something beyond self; how, quite like Harry, they thrive on searching for the new and unexpected and enjoy flying with the birds. As researchers and writers we sometimes experience this wonder when we become deeply fascinated by other people's worlds, struggle with questions, or are immersed in the joy of writing. The quality of "liberating laughter" speaks to the joy of losing ourselves in collective play with ideas, a serious play of bantering, associations, ridicule of established ways, and combinations of things few people may ordinarily think belong together. The quality of "activating drama" is about the self-adventures that idea work brings to people's lives. Imaginative ideas for the location of new oil fields, new architectural concepts, new feature articles, or how to win major litigation cases bring excitement, danger, opportunity, and purpose to people. A life totally void of idea work would be a life of boredom, stagnation, and indifference, the kind of life that the famous management engineer, F. W. Taylor, imagined for those workers whose jobs were subject to design by scientific management, the kind of work design that radically divorces mental activity from manual labor and rigidly prescribes the latter.

Great ideas are always both personal and relational. Great ideas are personal in the sense that, once aired, once launched from the realm of thought into the domain of discussion, they engage our deepest interests and launch individual and collective self-adventures where something is at stake. Participation in idea work for the Opera Building or a major oil discovery constitute experiences that people can dine out on, sources of pride that become their narrative capital. According to explorer Magnar Larsen at Statoil, who is widely considered the protagonist in the discovery of Norne, the northernmost oil discovery in the world at the time:

"It did not exactly hurt my professional reputation as a geologist. I was invited to give my opinion about oil discoveries elsewhere [...]. The biggest event for me as a geologist was Norne. I have been part of other discoveries, but this was the peak, it had so many spillover effects. It is important for me to have been part of something that mattered. I am a political person, so the societal significance of this was of great concern to me. I remember a person who had just become my leader said: 'This is going to stay with you'. He was right."

Great ideas are relational in the sense that they need to be shared, shaped, written into by many. Ideas live the strongest when they leave the cradle and become part of other people's purposes, ambitions, and hopes. The shape of a swan was one of many ideas drawn on in the construction of the Oslo Opera building, a concept that probably only a few people realize is deeply embedded in the final structure. Another concept, of "thresholds", was more open-ended and invitational, generous in the sense that it draws people in. Again in the words of Kjetil Trædal Thorsen:

> "If the project has the generous quality to begin with, so that it opens up for your own interpretations as you go – and generosity seems to be a very important theme in architecture – then it is as if the project develops itself. This means that you have found something, collectively, the very core of something that is this project's most important development potential."

THE THEORETICAL
CONTRIBUTION OF THE BOOK

Current creativity research increasingly tries to understand creativity as a collective phenomenon and a form of practice. Many scholars have pointed to an evident lack of focus on collective aspects of creativity in previous research (Sternberg and Lubart 1999, Kurtzberg and Amabile 2001, Sawyer 2006). As a response to this gap, research has increasingly tried to explore collective creativity in collaborative work (Hargadon and Sutton 1997, Drazin, Glynn and Kazanjian 1999, Hargadon and Bechky 2006, Mumford and Licuanan 2004, Sawyer 2006). Group collaboration has been a major focus in much of this research (Gilson and Shalley 2004), sometimes by means of interaction analysis (Murphy 2005, Sawyer and DeZutter 2009). Collective creativity has been portrayed, for example, as a relatively rare and fleeting phenomenon that occurs in moments of interaction characterized by four types of interactional behaviors: help-giving, help-seeking, reframing and reinforcing (Hargadon and Bechky 2006).

While these approaches are useful and necessary, there is still a need for research that explores creativity as unfolding in everyday work (Mumford and Licuanan 2004, Sawyer 2006). A focus on creativity in breakthrough moments, even allowing for a succession of these, does not seem sufficient. People also work on ideas when doing painstaking analysis; when they visualize preliminary understanding in sketching, mapping, or modeling; when they imagine future products and services, when they listen to a demanding client, or when they identify bias and unquestioned assumptions in previous efforts and subsequently generate entirely new ways of seeing (Locke, Golden-Biddle, & Feldman 2008). People also work with ideas when they connect analysis of particulars to broader wholes, whether disciplinary traditions, organizational purposes, or larger social struggles.

Talking about idea work rather than creativity allows one to take into account a range of efforts that may involve several work groups and specialists over time and that also span across projects. The concept of idea work allows us to consider sequences and iterations between a broad range of interdependent activities and mediating artifacts that in some way all contribute to developing, visualizing, preparing the ground for, and realizing ideas. The focus on idea work as a collective practice is inspired by the fledgling practice-based approach in organization studies (Schatzki and Knorr Cetina 2001, Gherardi 2006, Feldman and Orlikowski 2011), where the specifics of what people do in their everyday work is seen as vital for understanding communites of practice (Wenger 1998), learning (Nicolini, Gherardi, and Yanow 2003), knowing (Orlikowski 2000), or strategizing (Johnson, Melin, and Whittington 2003).

By introducing the term "idea work" we also aim to broaden the recognition of organizational practices considered creative. Creativity is often a term wrongfully reserved for artists and so-called creative industries. Also, the innovation literature has focused largely on the development of consumer goods, standardized services, or new high-tech solutions, rather than on creative practices, per se. In contrast to this focus, we suggest that idea work can take place more or less everywhere: in schools, banks, hospitals, consultancies, merchants, publishers, as well as university research laboratories – the list is almost endless. Thus we try to offer a language for talking about creative practice in many kinds of work and in all sectors of the economy.

We believe idea work is particularly relevant for making sense of the growing importance of project-based organizing (Lundin and Midler 1998, Sydow, Lindkvist, and DeFilippi 2004). Any project of some significance in organizations involves a certain amount of idea work, both in its conception (ideas pertaining to the challenges to be met and the problems to be solved) and completion (ideas on how to respond to unique user requests with the mix of services and capabilities one can offer).

What, then, about idea work versus knowledge work? Theories on knowing-in-practice (Nicolini, Gherardi, and Yanow 2003, Gherardi 2000) and knowledge creation (Nonaka and Takeuchi 1995), overlap with idea work in their focus on practice and in describing processes of "amplifying knowledge created by individuals" (Nonaka and Von Krogh 2009, p. 635), an inevitable part of working with ideas. But the concept of idea work is more directly tied to output and value than to resources. The creation of knowledge in the sense of "crystallizing and connecting it to an organization's knowledge system" (Nonaka and Von Krogh 2009, p. 635) is only a secondary purpose. Furthermore, idea work is not restricted to the elitist connotation and theoretical, disciplinary knowledge often attributed to knowledge work (Rylander 2009).

THE RESEARCH
BEHIND THE BOOK

This book is the direct result of a four-year research project called Idea Work that set out to understand sources of extraordinary ideas in leading organizations. See pages 34–35 for a presentation of the participating organizations that we use as cases for the study. The organizations all have a Scandinavian home-base. All of them are considered industry leaders in some sense, have demonstrated excellence in part of their history, and three of them have recently achieved recognition as international pioneers and practice leaders in innovation. Thus, as research cases, these six organizations provide a rich base for exploring extra-ordinary idea work. People in all six organizations have taken a strong interest in participating in the inquiry, in co-creating a language for idea work and in testing the insights in real work settings. The practical incentive of being able to improve work practice and not merely "being the object of a study" has been an important driver of the research[II]. A research approach closely involving practitioners is particularly important when studying idea work with highly specialized vocabu-lary and long time cycles. Exploration for gas and oil is the extreme case here, with project cycles that can span a decade and a vocabulary that will soon leave outsiders in the dark.

In direct response to the lack of practice-based approaches to creativity at work, the key questions in the Idea Work project were simple: What drives extraordinary creativity in everyday work? How do people do it? And how do we talk about it?

We have focused on practice – what people actually do when developing ideas in their everyday work – and on positive deviant practice – what work looks like when at its best. All organizations have problems and challenges with being creative; also all have moments when they achieve the extraordinary. By focusing on the extraordinary we try to energize the organization and point to possibilities, rather than limit learning to the averages of best practices.[III]

In order to develop a language of idea work we have systematically compared practices across the six organizations. What we share is based on observation, inter-views, feedback sessions, and active experimentation in these organizations. Briefly, this project has involved over 200 interviews, dozens of feedback events and work-shops, as well as more than 400 hours of observations, the latter also enabled by two PhDs who are both in the write-up phase of their research, one in an architecture firm (Aina Landsverk Hagen) and one in an oil company (Tord Fagerheim Mortensen).[IV]

Our analysis of data followed a so-called grounded theory research approach (Glaser and Strauss 1967, Charmaz 2006) involving practitioners in the six organizations. Central to any grounded approach is the move from empirical observations to theoretical categories via various forms of systematic coding and comparison. One challenge in such comparisons is to arrive at a format that allows for active involvement of practitioners. To accomplish this, we developed and used a new methodology with a deck of A5 cards for each organization, combining images (on the front) and brief texts (on the reverse side) to provide thin abstractions of tentative research findings (see Carlsen, Rudningen, and Mortensen 2012 for further details). Each card presented research findings in the form of distinct qualities for idea work at its best. Based on this, our analysis involved the following steps to identify and compare patterns of successful idea work practices within and across the six organizations:

1. From interviews, observation, and interactions, we developed a deck of cards for each of the six organizations, identifying qualities of extraordinary idea work and comprising eight to 24 cards per organization.

2. Within each organization the particular deck of cards was used to inter-act with practitioners in that organization. A typical way of doing this was to present the deck of cards in feedback sessions and have practitioners respond to the interpretations through various forms of scoring, prioriti-zation, and specification of follow-up actions. In addition, some of the insights were tested through work sessions addressing real challenges.

3. We compared the decks of cards across all six organizations asking the question: "What are the qualities of extraordinary idea work that people in the six different organizations have in common?"

The results of our analysis is the ten qualities of extraordinary idea work presented here. These are qualities that seem to be present in groups, projects, work processes and activities in which people are operating at their best. All ten qualities are not present at all times – only two or three may be observable in a single project – but all contribute in some way to the success of the organizations involved.

THE COLLABORATORS IN THIS BOOK

Ideas for architectural concepts and solutions: Snøhetta is a world- renowned architectural firm based in Oslo, Norway, and New York City. The company was established in the late 1980s with an ambition to integrate landscape architecture and architecture and started its road to fame by winning the competition for the Alexandria library. Later projects include the new Opera building in Oslo, the 9/11 Memorial Museum in New York and the renovation of Times Square. In 2010, Snøhetta had approximately 120 designers working on projects in Europe, Asia, and America. Snøhetta has won a series of international awards for its designs and was listed the most innovative architectural firm by Fast Company in 2011 *(see http://www.fastcompany.com/1738920/the-10-most-innovative-companies-in-architecture)*. Snøhetta's participation in Idea Work has taken place through projects in Oslo and New York, involving videotaped observations from ongoing projects and an ethnographic study by a Ph.D. student, Aina Landsverk Hagen.

Ideas for where to find oil and gas: Statoil is an international energy company, headquartered in Stavanger, Norway, with operations in 36 countries and 20,000 employees. Operating mainly within the oil and gas industry, Statoil has ambitious worldwide exploration activities with around 800 geoscientists working to develop acreage and new prospects for where hydrocarbons can be found. In 2011, Statoil discovered more oil than any other company and was regarded as the seventh most innovative company *(see http://money.cnn.com/magazines/fortune/mostadmired/2011/best_worst/best1.html)* in Fortune's list of most admired companies. Statoil's participation in Idea Work has been extensive, with over 100 interviews and eight workshops involving more than 300 explorers.

Ideas for development of new markets, services, and products in trading analytics: Point Carbon (as of 2010 acquired by Thompson Reuters and renamed Thompson Reuters Point Carbon) is a world-leading provider of independent news, analysis, and consulting services for global power, gas, and carbon markets. The firm has offices in Oslo (head office), Washington D.C., London, Tokyo, Beijing, Kiev, Hamburg, Zürich, and Malmö. Point Carbon was founded in 2000 and played a pioneering role in establishing the carbon market. The idea behind Point Carbon stemmed from research on environmental, energy, and resource management politics at the independent Fridtjof Nansen Institute in Norway, as well as from core competences in trading, journalism, and quantitative modeling. In Idea Work, the focus for Point Carbon has been on its portfolio of carbon market services, involving internal and external interviewing, some observation, and two workshops.

Ideas for legal strategies, solutions, and advice: Thommessen (Advokatfirmaet
Thommessen AS) is a leading corporate law firm in Norway, practicing in all areas
of commercial law. The firm has offices in Oslo, Bergen, and London and is also
the Norwegian member of Lex Mundi, the world's largest network of independent law firms. Thommessen was established in 1856, is consistently ranked first by
independent assessments, and was awarded Scandinavian Law Firm of the Year
(Chambers & Partners) in 2007–2009. The firm has a total staff of 290, of which 185
are lawyers. Acknowledging the importance of client interactions in Thommessen,
the focus on Idea Work there has been on further systematic learning from client
relationships through internal and external interviews and a series of subsequent
workshops. Reidar Gjersvik, co-editor of this book, did participant observation in
his three-year role as Chief Knowledge Officer at Thommessen.

Ideas for new products and services in banking: SpareBank 1 Alliance is the main
grouping of Norwegian savings banks and a leading provider of financial products
and services in the Norwegian market with around 10,000 employees. The banks
in the SpareBank 1 Alliance distribute the group's products and collaborate in key
areas such as brands, work processes, expertise development, IT operations and
system development. SpareBank 1 is known for the strong local engagement of
savings banks, reflected in local ownership and industrial development. Idea Work
has collaborated with the development function of SpareBank1 Alliance, including
interviews, attention to the corporate systems for idea development, and workshops
for generation of new ideas. The latter has also involved participation from technical
suppliers and clients.

Ideas for new feature articles: A-magasinet is the weekend magazine distributed
as a supplement to the leading Norwegian daily newspaper, *Aftenposten*. It is one of
Norway's largest weekend magazines with an established brand, a solid and stable
group of readers, and generally enjoys high recognition. The magazine features an
editorial line that tones down traditional lifestyle material, aims to be of value in
raising important societal concerns, and regularly includes long articles based on
investigative journalism. *A-magasinet* was not formally a full participant in the Idea
Work research project. Its involvement amounted to eight interviews, three brief
rounds of observations, archive studies, and a workshop.

Our research is informed by narrative methods of inquiry (Mishler 1986, Clandinin and Connelly 2000, Kohler-Riessman 2008), in our way of interviewing people, analyzing experiences across contexts and presenting them here. This means that we have tried to preserve context, by having people tell stories from their work or observe whole processes, used stories in our comparisons and also that we emphasize stories with flesh and blood characters in the ten qualities of extraordinary idea work.

Notwithstanding our protocols, readers should also be aware of the limitations of our research. The depth and duration of our involvement with the six organizations varied significantly – from over a hundred interviews and five years of engagement with hydrocarbon explorers, to a mere eight interviews and a few weeks of interactions with journalists. The difference between these outliers says something about those practices that are more opaque to outsiders, with exploration being the extreme case, with its highly specialized language and long project cycles. But it also underlines that we do not believe we have a full overview of the practices of idea work in the six organizations. Nobody has such knowledge, nor would it be possible to make such a claim: practices are always in process. Thus we do not claim that the patterns we highlight are necessarily stable over time or something recognizably homogeneous. Practices change all the time and seem different to different people. Thus, our ten qualities should not be taken as universal "truths". Not being positivists we do not expect to meet universal truths in our branch of social science. Rather, these qualities are ones that people in the partner organizations recognized as meaningful, which the researchers think provide a fair description, and with which we find resonance in other social science research. The robustness of the work is enhanced by the variance across context and the repeated involvement of practitioners in making comparisons. And the stories we tell will hopefully allow readers to make comparisons with their own worlds.

TO WHOM IS THIS BOOK ADDRESSED?

The book is aimed at managers, practitioners, researchers, and students of organizations who are interested in improving their outputs and their work processes: in short, people who do idea work and people interested in what makes organizations work well. Idea work takes place in every organization where prior experience and general knowledge need to be fitted and combined to meet unique demands and circumstances.

For some professions, the importance of idea work is obvious: Architects at Snøhetta cannot enter competitions without ideas for sketching new concepts. Geologists at Statoil searching for new gas and oil cannot develop prospects without some idea as to where the treasures are concealed underground. Likewise, journalists at weekend magazines compete with other weekend magazines based on ideas for feature articles, and lawyers depend on ideas when facing tough legal battles and while advising on complex financial restructurings, mergers, and strategies. In these settings, bad ideas, or an absence of ideas, simply means that one is not able to perform: competitive bids and legal cases would be lost. Oil would not be found. Readers would leave.

For others, the role of ideas in work is subtler, or more precisely put, so interwoven with daily work that we usually do not think of the practice as idea work. A farmer needs major ideas about how to achieve the best long-term harvest from the unique features of his or her soil, about regulations, cost considerations, and market conditions; but the farmer must also generate countless smaller ideas in solving everyday problems. A sports fisherman needs ideas about which flies to use under which conditions for what kind of prey and will thrive on exchanging such ideas with others. A cabin crew attendant needs ideas on how to handle difficult situations with schedule deviances or distressed, sick, or frightened passengers. Some of these ideas are developed and acted upon in split seconds; decisions are made in the blink of an eye. Taking the time to step back and say "I will now do idea work" might not actually help at all.

Thus, we shall reserve the term idea work for work with ideas that require organizational attention and interaction over time, where one needs to consider alternatives, and where major changes or new deliverables are at stake. This is still a broad concept; idea work is part of all important development work, most project-based work, and all work with sustained end-user interactions in problem solving, such as setting up curriculums for teachers or planning the development of a farm or developing new products and services for a bank. Idea work is relevant for everyone engaged in problem solving and development work and everyone who works with projects or tasks that may differ slightly from time to time.

HOW TO READ AND USE THE BOOK

Our ambition is that this book will be used by other researchers, for master's level teaching in universities but the book is also intended for practition-ers and professionals. In addition to the architects, lawyers, journalists, and other professionals that we discuss in the book, we think that students of management and innovation might benefit from a book this close to practice. The book is intended to be neither a "research-heavy" tome (although we have written such books elsewhere) nor a "pop" how-to text for one-minute managers or people with seven highly effective habits. The book aims to spur curiosity and make readers wonder about practices in their own organization and profession. It seeks to provide practical hints about how readers might approach issues of creativity and idea work in their own practice. Like us, you have probably spent more of your work-ing life in organizations characterized by a lack rather than a surfeit of imagination. We want to reverse the imbalance.

It will be possible for the reader to read this book from many angles and use it in any number of ways. If interested in architecture or explora-tion, you may pay special attention to Snøhetta's or Statoil's projects. If you want to read social or organization science, you may focus on the descriptions and theory of the qualities of idea work. Other starting points may be through approaches to creative work practice (what do professionals do?), or through practical tips on how to promote a given quality in your organization, or even as a tool for further research. We envisage the book as a tool for creativity of all sorts; in particular, it can be used as a stimulus for creativity sessions in organizations where analogies, extensions, and approximations are work-shopped, discussed, and materialized. To make this kind of usage feasible, we have engaged closely with everyday practice, borrowing examples from leading idea workers and basing our descriptions on solid research, taking the reader backstage into real situations and offering practical tips, compelling stories, and, above all, accessible, engaging, and thought-provoking insights.

WHAT ABOUT ARTISTRY?

As a way to further exemplify and expand our understanding of extra-ordinary idea work, we have included small snippets from the work of one or more great artists in all chapters. While many of these artists may be seen to represent the prototypical lonely genius that possesses qualities of artistic creativity and seemingly directly opposes of our concept of idea work, we beg to differ. In a provocative sense, one could understand individual artistry as the label for a collective practice of engagement with vital traditions of ideas. We do not aim to provide a full analysis of artistic practice. Instead of following the usual route of starting with the lonely genius and imposing lessons learned on organizations, the intention here is to play with the inverse: Is there an affinity between the patterns of collective practice that we have seen in extraordinary idea work and the work of great artists? The work of Bob Dylan will be revisited several times in these snippets, reflecting his highly acclaimed artistry, the seemingly individual nature of his work (if Dylan can be regarded to be doing collec-tive idea work, who could not?), and our own fascination with his work.[v]

REFERENCES

Amabile, T. M. (1996). *Creativity in Context.* New York, NY: Westwood Press.

Carlsen, A., Rudningen, G. and Mortensen, T. (2012). Playing the cards. On the aesthetics of making research-cogenerative. Paper in review, an earlier version was presented at the Third International Process Symposium in Corfu, Greece 16–18 June, 2011.

Charmaz, K. (2006). *Constructing Grounded Theory: A Practical Guide through Qualitative Analysis.* Thousand Oaks, CA: Sage.

Clandinin, D. J. and Connelly, F. M. (2000). *Narrative Inquiry: Experience and Story in Qualitative Research.* San Francisco, CA: Jossey-Bass Publishers.

Coldevin, G. H., Carlsen, A., Clegg, S., Antonacopoulou, E. og Pitsis, T. (2013). Idea work in organizations. Towards a practice-based approach. Artikkel i reviewprosess.

Cook, S.D.N. and Brown, J. S. (1999). Bridging epistemologies: The generative dance between organizational knowledge and organizational knowing. *Organization Science* 10(4): 381–400.

Csikszentmihalyi, M. (1996). *Creativity. Flow and the Psychology of Discovery and Innovation.* New York, NY: Harper-Collins.

Csikszentmihalyi, M. (1999). Implications of a systems perspective for the study of creativity. I R.J. Sternberg (red.), *Handbook of Creativity.* (pp. 313-328). Cambridge, UK: Cambridge University Press.

Drazin, R., Glynn. M. A. and Kazanjian, R. K. (1999). Multilevel theorizing about creativity in organizations: A sensemaking perspective. *Academy of Management Review* 24(2): 286–307.

Elden, M. og Levin, M. (1991). Co-generative learning: Bringing participation into action research. I W.F. Whyte (red.), *Participatory Action Research* (pp. 127–142). Newbury Park, CA: Sage.

Feldman, M.S. and Orlikowski, W. J. (2011). Theorizing practice and practicing theory. *Organization Science* 22(5): 1240-1253.

Flyvbjerg, B. (2002). *Making Social Science Matter: Why Social Inquiry Fails and How It Can Succeed Again.* Cambridge, UK: Cambridge University Press.

Gherardi, S. (2000). Practice-based theorizing on learning and knowing in organizations. *Organization* 7(2): 211-223.

Gherardi, S. (2006). *Organizational Knowledge: The Texture of Workplace Learning.* Oxford: Blackwell.

Gilson, L.L. and Shalley, C. E. (2004). A little creativity goes a long way: An examination of teams' engagement in creative processes. *Journal of Management* 30(4), 453–470.

Glaser, B.G. and Strauss, A. L. (1967). *The Discovery of Grounded Theory.* Chicago, IL: Aldine.

Hargadon, A. (2003). *How Breakthroughs Happen.* Boston, MA: Harvard Business School Press.

Hargadon, A. B. and Bechky, B. A. (2006). When collections of creatives become creative collectives: A field study of problem solving at work. *Organization Science* 17(4): 484-500.

Hargadon, A. B. and Sutton, R. I. (1997). Technology brokering and innovation in a product development firm. *Administrative Science Quarterly* 42(4): 716-749.

Johnson, G., Melin, L., and Whittington, R. (2003). Special issue on micro-strategy and strategizing: Towards an activity-based view. *Journal of Management Studies* 40(1): 3–22.

Koestler, A. (1964/1989). *The Act of Creation.* London: Penguin.

Kohler-Riessman, C. (2008). *Narrative Methods for the Human Sciences.* Thousand Oaks, CA: Sage.

Kurtzberg, T. R. and Amabile, T. M. (2001). From Guilford to creative synergy: Opening the black box of team level creativity. *Creativity Research Journal* 13(3–4): 285–294.

Locke, K., Golden-Biddle, K. and Feldman, M. (2008). Making doubt generative: Rethinking the role of doubt in the research process. *Organization Science* 19(6): 907–918.

Lundin, R. and Midler, C. (1998). *Projects as Arenas for Renewal and Learning Processes.* Boston, MA: Kluwer.

Mishler, E., G. (1986). *Research Interviewing. Context and Narrative.* Cambridge, MA: Harvard University Press.

Mumford, M.D. and Licuanan, B. (2004). Leading for innovation: Conclusions, issues, and directions. *Leadership Quarterly* 15(1): 163–171.

Murphy, K.M. (2005). Collaborative imagining: The interpretive use of gestures talk and graphic representation in architectural practice. *Semiotica* 1(4) 113–145.

Nicolini, D., Gherardi, S. and Yanow, D. (2003). *Knowing in Organizations: A Practice-Based Approach.* London: M. E. Sharpe.

Nonaka, I. og Takeuchi, H. (1995). *The Knowledge Creating Company: How Japanese Companies Create the Dynamics of Innovation.* New York, NY: Oxford University Press.

Nonaka, I. and Von Krogh, G. (2009). Tacit knowledge and knowledge conversion: Controversy and advancement in organizational knowledge creation theory. *Organization Science* 20(3): 635–652.

Orlikowski, W.J. (2000). Using technology and constituting structures: A practice lens for studying technology in organizations. *Organization Science* 11(4): 404–428.

Peirce, C. S. (1878/1958). How to make our ideas clear. In P. Wiener (red.), *Charles S. Peirce: Selected Writings* (s. 113–141). Toronto, Dover.

Rylander, A. (2009). Design thinking as knowledge work: Epistemological foundations and practical implications. *Design Management Journal* 4(1): 7–19.

Sawyer, R. K. (2006). *Explaining Creativity: The Science of Human Innovation.* New York, NY: Oxford University Press.

Sawyer, R.K., and DeZutter, S. (2009). Distributed creativity: How collective creations emerge from collaboration. *Psychology of Aesthetics, Creativity, and the Arts* 3(2): 81–92.

Schatzki, T. and Knorr Cetina, K. (2001) *The Practice Turn in Contemporary Theory.* London: Routledge.

Spreitzer, G. and Sonenshein, S. (2004). Toward the construct definition of positive deviance. *American Behavioral Scientist* 47(6): 828–47.

Sternberg, R. J. and Lubart, T. I. (1999). The concept of creativity: Prospects and paradigms. I R. J. Sternberg (red.), *Handbook of Creativity* (s. 3–15). New York, NY: Cambridge University Press.

Sydow, J., Lindkvist, L. and DeFillippi, R. (2004): Project-based organizations, embeddedness and repositories of knowledge. *Organization Studies* 25(9): 1475–1489.

Wenger, E. (1998). *Communities of Practice: Learning, Meaning, and Identity.* Cambridge, UK: Cambridge University Press.

NOTES

I. The four categories may be seen as a conceptual relative to Amabile's (1996) three-component model of creativity. Amabile differentiates between 1) creative skills or creative thinking, 2) expertise, and 3) task motivation. A full comparison is outside the scope here, but roughly we can say that the affective qualities of extraordinary idea work (daring to imagine, craving wonder, and activating drama) correspond to and extend the concept of task motivation. Likewise, the interwoven qualities of idea work (prepping and zooming out) correspond to Amabile's expertise component. The largest difference in our conception here is that we have identified a range of both controversial (generative resistance, liberating laughter, and punk production) and material (double rapid prototyping and getting physical) qualities of idea work that go beyond the notion of creative skills (which normally do not recognize issues of power) or creative thinking (which is overly cognitively oriented).

II. The practical interest from the participating organizations is important not only because it ensures engagement in interpretation of findings and co-creation of a language for idea work. Practical interest also serves to set up arenas where the emergent conceptions can be tested by, for example, designing and carrying out workshops on real challenges, workshops that are informed by the ten identified qualities of extraordinary idea work. Statoil is probably the case organization with the most direct practical utilization of the results with eight two-day workshops engaging over 300 explorers and disseminating findings to more than 800 explorers. In 2010, Statoil's chief geologist publicly attributed the increased discovery rate to the Idea Work collaboration (*A-magasinet* 2010 (10): pp. 8–18: Seriøs kreativitet [Serious Creativity]). The following year, seven impact discoveries were made, totaling a resource increase that amounted to more than any other oil company in the world. We do not claim causality here. At best, the Idea Work project has had an indirect influence on these discoveries. The point is simply to illustrate that our research has benefitted from being close to high-impact practice.

III: This is a research strategy that emphasizes learning from positive deviant cases (in contrast to learning from problems alone) and strives to understand the basis for extraordinary performances, practices, and relationships. It is a research strategy with many roots, now broadly taken up in positive psychology and positive organizational scholarship (Spreitzer and Sonenshein 2004). We have used it to systematically look for peak moments in interactions and to try to understand dynamics in situations and projects that were in some sense extraordinary. We also see it as a constructive way of interacting with people in the field in terms of establishing trust and inviting people into joint activities of reflection. Asking people about their successes energizes the conversation and may convey an attitude of "we are here to learn from and with you", rather than "we are here to learn from your failures and find out how you can improve in your work". Also, paradoxically, talking about positive deviant events seems to open the ground for also discussing failures. The interviewee is enlisted comparing the positive deviant situations and projects with the negative ones rather than overlooking the latter. A typical interview in the Idea Work research project would start by having people identify and tell stories of success projects and peak moments. Here we rely on narrative approaches to interviewing where people's experiences are put in context, where the voice of interviewees is preserved and their experiences made part of a coherent story (Mishler 1986, Kohler-Riessman 2008). Next we would try to engage interviewees in various forms of comparisons, e.g., "What is the difference between a peak moment/a success project and those that amount to little? What distinguishes an extraordinary team session/ team practice/team leadership from the mediocre ones?" A third section of interviews would deal more systematically with causalities, for example: "What could you to bring about the positive deviant experiences more often. What enables or stifles extraordinary idea work?"

	Observations	Interviews	Interaction events	Archives
SpareBank 1-alliansen	Limited: ca. 20+ hours, mainly review meetings	12 employees, eight users	Five workshops, of which one also involved suppliers	Media articles, project records, policy documents, web
Thommessen	Extensive: three years with researcher in participant observation role as chief knowledge officer	10 + 8 employees, six clients	Six workshops focused on learning from clients, all with feedback sessions	Case material, internal knowledge management systems and archives, media articles, web
Point Carbon	Limited: 20+ hours, two meetings and a handful of site visits	20 employees, eight clients	Two two-day workshops with feedback sessions	Media articles, project records, policy documents, web
Snøhetta	Extensive: 200+ hours (project meetings, client meetings, site visits)	22 employees	Four feedback sessions	Media articles, project records, books, web
Statoil	Extensive: 250+ hours, (work sessions, project meetings, presentations, review meetings)	110+ employees at all levels, including the CEO	Eight two-day workshops, all including feedback sessions	Media articles, project records, internal discovery stories, regional overviews, data (logs, seismic) policy documents
A-magasinet	Limited: three meetings, five brief visits	eight employees	One feedback session	Work in progress, finished articles, web, a few policy documents

V. Bob Dylan is one of the more recognized artists of our time. Not merely a song and dance man, he is also a Nobel Prize candidate, Oscar and Pulitzer Prize winner, recipient of the president of the United States' highest award, the Medal of Freedom, as well as a dazzling producer of music and lyrics from new ideas, texts, and metaphors so strong that they have become part of our daily lives; he is one of the defining voices of our time and custodian of some of the most vital traditions in vernacular American music, someone who still manages to renew himself nightly in performance, taking risks with repertoire, arrangements, and accompanists. Stewart Clegg has had a long-standing fascination with the work of Dylan ever since he first heard him in 1962, fifty years ago at the time of writing. What was fascinating was that, in an age of forgeries and fakes, this seemed to be the real thing, albeit in masquerade. The fascination has wavered at times but has never lapsed, even as Dylan tested the loyalty of the most dedicated fans with some of his recorded idea works and movies. With Dylan as his teacher, Clegg learned to become a sociologist as much as with his more formal mentors; with Dylan he learned the importance of rhythm in writing and the cadences of composition; with Dylan he learned appreciation of art that takes us where it will, whether into the gospels, or the back roads of an East Texas populated with martyrs, Brownsville girls, and a movie starring Gregory Peck.

PREPPING
WHY EVERY ORGANIZATION SHOULD HAVE AN UNCLE SAM

TORD F. MORTENSEN[1], ARNE CARLSEN, ARNE LINDSETH BYGDÅS[2], STEWART CLEGG AND REIDAR GJERSVIK

prep·ping |
The practice of carefully preparing, building, and revitalizing knowledge in a way that maximizes its potential for effective use in the moment of creation.

Erik Samuelsen is something of an institution at Thommessen, a leading law firm that has won consecutive awards as the best in Scandinavia. Erik has worked at Thommessen for 40 years, resigned as partner in 2012, and now works part time on special cases for the management. No other lawyer at the Oslo office of the organization has argued more cases before the Supreme Court, and he is renowned both inside and outside the organization. Insiders cherish him for his capacity to provide an overview, his pleasant manner and his willingness and ability to contribute to the cases of others. People at Thommessen call him simply "Uncle Sam". When one meets him, his open, friendly face above the spotless lawyer's suit and tie is striking. His is an outward-directed, warm intelligence, one that shows interest and provides thoughtful answers in clear, direct language. But there is no cushioning in Erik's reasoning. He might tell you to be a bit more forward-leaning in your work on a case, to find a new angle, to forget shortcuts, or to go back and do your homework better before the conversation can continue. Surely, anyone would want an uncle like that. But what does he *do* so well?

> "When I get involved in a Supreme Court case, the first thing I do is appoint a process committee, which may be regarded as a colloquium or project group where I am the project manager. The client's lawyer is also included in this group. We start our work by thoroughly discussing with the client what he or she wants, why we should go to court, why he or she believes we can do this, what the background reasons are, and what has happened."

[1]Department of Psychology, University of Oslo, [2]The Work Research Institute in Oslo

"A common case in court is typically 95 percent a matter of facts. The law is just an instrument you add afterwards, except in very special cases. The facts are extremely important. You need to have this clarified before you go on to the good ideas. You must have stamina to go through all the nitty-gritty details of the case matter, and it is nice to have people available around you who can help you in this and also to reflect about what is really at stake here. When the facts of the matter are established, then you can sit down and come up with the good ideas, and this can be done in several ways. One perspective is to find a legal approach; what does the law say about this matter, what claims can we propose, where do we want to go with this? But even though you have set up a skeleton of legal arguments and propositions, it turns out that there is still a painstaking job to be done in finding and digging into all the relevant sources, the factors that the court will take into consideration when they pass judgment. Sources of law are what the judge has to draw from when he or she sits down to make a ruling. Another possibility is to analyze the arguments presented by the opposing party. We then go through their arguments and dissect them to find out what the opponent thinks, and try to stay ahead with counter-arguments and draw up a skeleton or brief to use against the other party's contentions. A third approach is to come up with bright ideas for presenting material, both facts and legal material. But also: Are there any holes in the arguments that we have not seen? Is there something new, something innovative, that we can do about this?"

Uncle Sam illustrates that prepping is simply the most basic practice in any form of professional idea work. Without the background knowledge and preparation of input facts and opinions about a matter, there is simply nothing to combine to generate valuable new ideas. Nobody wants a lawyer or an architect who is creative but who lacks a solid base to stand on. Explorers call it "prospects without legs" – ideas that, when questioned only a little bit, fall to the ground immediately.

MAKING THE KNOWLEDGE AND THE ANALOGIES COLLECTIVELY AVAILABLE

Prepping is about getting the right knowledge ready for combination at the right time, at the moment of association. This includes general education and experiences from previous cases as well as more specific elements of activating knowledge through specific cases and questions.

One way of viewing prepping is to think of a collective field of immediate, vivid attention that needs to be *charged* with necessary input, as opposed to fragmented and disjointed bits of information and experiences. Such charging is not about building huge repositories of data and mapping the knowledge of employees. To do that is a mistake in knowledge management – to think that we can objectify tacit knowing into formal knowledge. This is a misguided illusion and an error on which billions of dollars have been wasted to very little effect. The phrase "if organizations only knew what they know" is fundamentally mistaken. Most of what we know will not need to be applicable for a particular idea. It should simply be dismissed. We know through knowing, not knowledge – whether it is stored in a database, file, or book – it is only in the moment of knowledge's being known, that is, when enacted knowledge, that it has purpose. Otherwise it is as dead as yesterday's newspapers, an archive of arcane knowledge that is rendered useless by no one's knowing.

When building and activating the facts of prepping, when charging the field, knowing is something that occurs in the moment of creative interaction, most often within a group of people; thus, enhancing the range of associations of possible raw material is vital. Hence, we need to have knowledge available in ways that enable access to "the final moment of association". And this is where seasoned idea workers, like Uncle Sam, come in: their memory functions as an institutional filter for collecting current relevancies and relating them to phenomena, people, and things that have passed this way before. Uncle Sam works as a living reminder of the value of prepping but he is also a living repository of knowing, a fount of knowledge, whose gentle ways and genuine interest lower the barrier to engagement. In this sense, it is not his ability to come up with ideas himself that makes him so valuable; it is rather his knowing, which works as a spur on others' cases. Uncle Sam puts people on the right track.

"How good people are at coming up with ideas varies considerably. There are many good thinkers here in this house, thinkers who possess a pool of good ideas. I'm more of a director, the one staging the scene: 'What do you think about this, boys and girls?' I'm fairly good at influencing others to come up with good ideas, but I am not a lighthouse myself. If I feel that I am really into a factual and juridical borderland, then I sometimes think that 'this was extraordinarily smart,' 'wow, this sounds totally crazy, but maybe...' or 'that was a damn good angle we have to think more about...' I have the advantage that I have 40 years of experience. So I can hand out tasks to the teams: 'Search a bit more up that alley'. When the kinds of cases that I have been involved with since I was 27 come up, my ideas mainly lie in the things I've been part of: 'But hell, in 1982, we did it this way; let's try it that way instead'."

Establishing the facts is one of the key ingredients in prepping, but not everything. After getting all the details together and out in the open, they need to be subjected to alternative solutions. It is clear that by consulting Uncle Sam one gets access to a repository of similar and not so similar cases with which one can reconsider present facts – his experience provides many analogies for current concerns. As voiced by another Thommessen senior partner:

"Creating analogies is about creating a collective setting where the problem is framed and knowledge is shared. That is the difference between success and failure. [...] To get a grip on aspects of the case that lie under the surface, in the periphery. Analogies offered by others bring critical aspects out into the daylight. Breadth is key here. Sometimes when I meet lawyers from smaller firms in court, I can just tell that their preparation suffers from not having been subjected to analogies from more distant legal areas."

TOUCHING ROCKS, REVIVIFYING & RE-SYNTHESIZING DATA, STAGING LONG CONVERSATIONS

Prepping is a decisive major ingredient in oil exploration. "The best explorers have simply seen the most geology" is an oft-repeated adage in Statoil. An explorer at the Houston offices talks about the importance of immersing oneself in geology by imagining being underground, touching rocks, and seeing outcrops:

> "It is a question of imagination. I mean, this is why you've got to get out there on the outcrops in Utah and South Africa and crawl on those rocks and stare at them for another week, and draw pictures of them and keep going back to the raw reality, over and over and over. So that this will just get embedded in that – you know – that great unconscious supercomputer, and it's there – not on demand, but it will appear when needed – to help you."

Magnar Larsen, a long-timer at Statoil's Harstad office in Nordland county, is in many ways a local Uncle Sam. Magnar was central in one of the major findings on the Norwegian shelf, the Norne field, which in 1991 was the northernmost discovery in Norway. The backdrop was a series of 9–10 dry wells in the area. The exploration license was about to expire, and the area would soon have to be turned back to the authorities if no discovery was confirmed. Magnar and his exploration team sat down and undertook the tedious task of going through all the dry wells again, revivifying and re-synthesizing old data to compile a new file for each well in one large folder. The new ideas for where oil could be found (and eventually about 500 million barrels was found) emerged from that detailed prepping. A parallel case is the more recent Skrugard discovery in 2011 (see also the chapter "Daring to Imagine") where the fast interpretation of new seismic data was enabled by a recent analysis of all previous wells in the area. When the new data showed a "double flat spot", comparisons with all previous double flat spots in the area could be done instantly.

Prepping often involves revisiting old cases, bringing up some data or pieces of knowledge that, when seen with new eyes, might yield breakthrough ideas. It is about consulting old files, reviewing them again, taking the effort to do tedious work but with an open mind. A typical opportunity for new prepping in exploration is to synthesize data across old license borders, seeing connections that were previously missed.

People can win through prepping simply because they have more stamina, are more thorough than others, and bring up new details that turn out to be decisive for the quality of ideas. Such details are regular features in the investigative journalism at *A-magasinet*, for example, in revealing dubious health products, fraud in marketing, or turning public opinion in a case against an ambulance driver accused of racism. In the latter case, the journalist in question spent four weeks closely scrutinizing the records of police interviews of all those involved.

At Snøhetta, architects talk about the long journey that needs to be travelled before one enters the creative rooms; the decisive concept that underpins the design and building of the Norwegian Opera resulted from a very long conversation – almost two months of joint work on references, user requirements, aesthetics, commercial limits, technical matters, turning the stones over and over again.

In all these cases, the winning practice seems to be 1) to charge a group of people with all the small and large bits of knowledge needed to generate new ideas and 2) to repeatedly discuss alternative ways of combining them: alternative case strategies, alternative conceptions for a building, alternative prospects for where oil can be found. *Then*, and only then, are you are ready to reach the decisive combination. This is called prepping.

PREPPING IN RESEARCH

Graham Wallas, frequently credited as the grandfather of creativity research, distinguished four stages in the creative process (Wallas 1926): preparation, incubation, illumination, and verification. A curious observation is that minimal research has been done on the processes that can be categorized under the preparation and verification stages of the model (Hélie and Sun 2010). We know little about the processes leading up to the act of creation, only that it often takes a long time to achieve a level of breakthrough expertise, typically ten years (e.g., Weisberg 2003).

In Wallas' framework, the preparation stage is wide and deep, it is a combination of "the whole process of intellectual education" (p. 82) and the active decision of the creative person to" 'put his mind on' to a chosen subject [...] The educated man has also acquired, by the effort of observation and memorizing, a body of remembered facts and words which gives him a wider range in the final moment of association" (p. 83).

In organization studies, the literatures that come closest to providing insights into prepping are probably those inquiring into knowledge creation (see for example Majchrzak, More and Samer 2012) and knowledge brokering. An example of the latter: Hargadon and Sutton (1997) described practices for knowledge brokering in the design firm IDEO (and also refer to the Thomas Edison Lab) as a cross-pollination between disparate industries based on network position and practices for making knowledge available through *acquisition* (e.g., reading about or doing projects for other firms) *storage* (e.g., through artifacts and records from projects or information hubs like Uncle Sam) and *retrieval* (e.g., through analogues and associated sharing and connecting). These practices parallel the concept of prepping, both in terms of making knowledge available for combination and in the emphasis on analogical reasoning.

Another key source, one that speaks more indirectly to prepping, is the pioneering work of Karl Weick on imagination. Weick (2006) underlines the importance of not locking our understanding into predefined categories and schemas. To imagine valuable ideas, we need to develop knowledge by acquaintance rather than by description. Prepping, done properly, is a way to be in repeated direct contact with experiences and primary data so that our understanding is bottoms-up and stimuli-driven, rather than top-down and schema-driven.

BORROWING FROM SHAKESPEARE AND DISSECTING CORPSES

"The greatest genius is the most indebted man", the forefather of pragmatism, Ralph Waldo Emerson (1850/1995: p. 134), said more than 150 years ago. The combination of ideas and facts that come from prepping always implies borrowing things from elsewhere, internally and externally. Sometimes such borrowing and incubation can take almost a lifetime. We might think of the great *Love and Theft* album by Bob Dylan, with its depth and complexity, with borrowings from almost everywhere: literature – Shakespeare, Mark Twain, Tennessee Williams, F. Scott Fitzgerald – as well as Minstrel Shows, blues, old movies, all evoking and drawing on a sense of an America that has perished except on celluloid and in the imagination. Without prepping on a career-defining scale, such art is unimaginable.

At some stage, most prepping will have a strong visceral dimension. Touching rocks, performing, or otherwise literally getting one's hands dirty are all equivalents to prepping that engage the body. Like many other artists, the Swedish Nobel laureate Tomas Tranströmer is known for rewriting his poems again and again and again. The mere exchange of a word is not done in a marginal note, but by rewriting the entire poem (Bugge 2011). Another example of such embodiment can be seen in the work of Leonardo Da Vinci, who found it decisive, when studying the human body, to move from mere drawings to physically handling corpses in varying degrees of decay:

>

"And you, who say that it would be better to watch an anatomist at work than to see these drawings, you would be right, if it were possible to observe all the things which are demonstrated in such drawings in a single figure, in which you, with all your cleverness, will not see nor obtain knowledge of more than some few veins, to obtain a true and perfect knowledge of which I have dissected more than ten human bodies, destroying all the other members, and removing the very minutest particles of the flesh by which these veins are surrounded, without causing them to bleed, excepting the insensible bleeding of the capillary veins; and as one single body would not last so long, since it was necessary to proceed with several bodies by degrees, until I came to an end and had a complete knowledge; this I repeated twice, to learn the differences. And if you should have a love for such things you might be prevented by loathing, and if that did not prevent you, you might be deterred by the fear of living in the night hours in the company of those corpses, quartered and flayed and horrible to see. And if this did not prevent you, perhaps you might not be able to draw so well as is necessary for such a demonstration; or, if you had the skill in drawing, it might not be combined with knowledge of perspective; and if it were so, you might not understand the methods of geometrical demonstration and the method of the calculation of forces and of the strength of the muscles; patience also may be wanting, so that you lack perseverance. As to whether all these things were found in me or not, the hundred and twenty books composed by me will give verdict Yes or No. In these I have been hindered neither by avarice nor negligence, but simply by want of time. Farewell."
(Leonardo da Vinci in Barron, Montuori, and Barron 1997, pp. 178–179)

TIPS FOR PRACTICE

1. *Take your time:* Have the persistence to go through data and old files, or talk to lead users yet one more time, even when people might have done so before. Depth of thinking in prepping enhances retrieval in "the final moment of association".

2. *Stage long conversations:* Five persons can create considerably more associations than can one. When encountering critical challenges that need fresh ideas, try and fill a room with people whose knowing will unlock different domains.

3. *Cultivate and use your "Uncle Sam's":* Most organizations have long-timers with extremely valuable knowledge that may be activated when developing new ideas. Recognize their knowledge, treat them with respect, and bring them into your process. Sometimes, a quick question and a thank you will do.

4. *Physical cues:* Immerse the group in artifacts such as books, similar products/objects to those that you think that you are trying to create – or newspaper stories, music, and sketches. Such cues can all trigger reactivation of knowing learnt from previous cases or from other domains.

5. *Frame problems and challenges abstractly:* In a collective setting, the greater the extent to which you can make the issues stand apart from the specifics of the particular case, the easier it will be for your colleagues to be able to know how to enhance associations and analogues.

6. *Practice communicating the essence, the gist of an idea:* To facilitate understanding of and commitment to the challenge in focus, try to drive home the essence of what you know in as immediate way as possible.

7. *Affective cues*: Hot thoughts are more memorable than cold thoughts. Don't shy away from heated discussions and projects that resonate with passion. Creative processes that acknowledge and utilize both negative and positive affect open a larger repository of knowledge at the point of association. Your passion can alert my knowing and vice versa.

8. *Active rehearsal:* Repeated rehearsal is the memory enhancing principle par excellence. Make sure you go over the stuff you are working on repeatedly. Only then will you be able to improvise on the fly.

THINGS TO AVOID

Trying to be creative without basic knowledge. Believing that having looked at the details ten or even only two years ago will be sufficient. Lack of persistence. Not taking the effort to go through the files and information you already have before asking for new ones. Not involving others so as to increase the potential for original combinations and associations. Prepping without any physical artifacts, markings, or visual traces that can keep bits and pieces alive and vivid for future combination. Not subjecting the established facts to alternative storylines, cases, metaphors, hypotheses, or explanations. Staying too close to in-family models and previous cases.

RESOURCES FOR
LEARNING AND INSPIRATION

Barron, F., Montuori, A. and Barron, A. (eds.) (1997). *Creators on Creating.* New York, NY: Jeremy P. Tarcher/Penguin. [For accounts of prepping (and other things) in the work of highly creative individuals.]

Bugge, H. L. B. (2011). NRK P2 podcast: Tomas Tranströmer interpreted by Hanna Louise Bovim Bugge, http://itunes.apple.com/no/podcast/nrk-p2-diktafon/id327894885. Last visited August 2012.

Carlsen, A. and Dutton, J. (eds.) (2011). *Research Alive. Exploring Generative Moments of Doing Qualitative Research.* Copenhagen: Copenhagen Business School Press. [For accounts of prepping in conducting qualitative research. See particularly chapters by Pratt and Johnson and Feldman.]

Dylan, B. (2001). *Love and Theft.* New York, NY: CBS Records.

Emerson, R. W. (1850/1995). *Representative Men.* P. Schirmeister (ed.) New York, NY: Marsilio Publishers. [A classical text on individual self-reliance and the social character of genius from the forefather of pragmatism.]

Hargadon, A. and Sutton, R.I. (1997). Technology brokering and innovation in a product development firm. *Administrative Science Quarterly* 42: 716-749 [A classical article in the knowledge brokering literature with high relevance for prepping.]

Hargadon, A. (2003). *How Breakthroughs Happen.* Boston, Ma: Harvard Business School Press. [This book broadens the theory of knowledge brokering first offered in the 1997 paper above, summarizing ten years of research on creative recombination of ideas within and across firms and industries.]

Hélie, S. and Sun, R. (2010). Incubation, insight, and creative problem solving: A unified theory and a connectionist model. *Psychological Review*, 117(3), 994-1024. [This paper synthesizes some of the psychological basis for understanding prepping and is particularly strong in terms of unifying contributions on incubation, insight, and the activation of implicit knowledge.]

Koestler, A. (1964/1989). *The Act of Creation.* Harmondsworth: Penguin. [Koestler's book preceded much later work on knowledge combination and is particularly strong on the mechanisms for bi-sociation; developing ideas by combining seemingly incompatible models, concepts or assumptions.]

Majchrzak, A., More, P.H.B. and Samer, F. (2012). Transcending knowledge differences in cross-functional teams. *Organization Science* 23(4): 951-970 [A path-breaking recent contribution within knowledge creation theory that compares practices in three crossfunctional teams. The authors identified practices for transcending knowledge differences – rather than traversing them – through voicing of solution fragments and rapid co-creation of intermediate scaffolds.]

Mortensen, T. (forthcoming 2013). *Unplugged Creativity.* Doctoral Dissertation in preparation at the Department of Psychology, University of Oslo. [A rich account of prepping in the idea work of hydrocarbon exploration.]

Tsoukas, H. (1993). Analogical reasoning and knowledge generation in organisation theory. *Organization Studies*, 14: 323-346. [A classical paper on analogical reasoning.]

Wallas, G. (1926). *The Art of Thought.* London: J. Cape. [This is a classic book on creativity that is explicit about the importance and mechanisms of prepping.]

Weick, K.E. (2006). The role of imagination in the organizing of knowledge. European Journal of Information Systems 15(5): 446–52 [One of several articles where Weick attends to the relationship between knowing and imagination in organizations.]

Weisberg, R.W. (2003). Case studies of innovation: Ordinary thinking, extraordinary outcomes. In L. V. Shavinina (ed.). *International Handbook of Innovation.* (pp. 203-247). New York, NY: Elsevier Science. [Provides a fine updated intro to the 10-year rule and other features of the "ordinariness" of preparing for extraordinary idea work.]

EXERCISES

1. What are the two necessary key elements in prepping? Describe what could go wrong if one of them is missing.

2. Do you think prepping is at odds with "thinking outside the box"? Is it possible to overdo prepping?

3. What do you think are the key questions to successful prepping?

4. Looking back at your own most successful idea work – whether alone or in projects – what characterized the prepping leading up to the decisive combination of knowledge?

5. Looking ahead towards future idea work projects, describe as concretely as possible how you could better organize your prepping in a specific project.

6. Looking across to other qualities of idea work: In which ways can getting physical enable prepping? What is the relationship between prepping and zooming out? Between prepping and craving wonder?

7. Looking to the theory on creativity, innovation, or knowledge creation: Can you think of contributions, concepts, and papers that could be categorized under the heading "prepping" but are not necessarily placed there today?

ZOOMING OUT
WHY SEEING THE BIG PICTURE MATTERS TO YOUR IDEAS

ARNE CARLSEN, STEWART CLEGG,
REIDAR GJERSVIK AND TORD F. MORTENSEN[1]

zoom·ing out |
Stepping back from immersion in data and analysis of ideas of particulars to big picture thinking, letting go of details, and seeking the simplifying core.

"As places animate the ideas and feelings of persons who attend them, these same ideas and feelings animate the places on which attention has been bestowed, and the movements of this process – inward toward facets of the self, outward towards aspects of the external world, alternately both together – cannot be known in advance. When places are actively sensed, the physical landscape becomes wedded to the landscape of the mind, to the roving imagination, and where the latter may lead is anybody's guess."

Keith Basso, (1996: p. 55) *Wisdom Sits in Places*

What is the common denominator between a really good presentation of a prospect for where oil can be found, writing a good feature article, developing a new cash management service, creating a convincing strategy for winning a legal case, formulating an analysis of a new climate change policy, and designing a prospect for an architectural competition?

The answer is fairly simple but non-trivial: small ideas are connected to larger ones. The oil prospect starts from an understanding of the entire basin. The feature article connects to larger stories of culture, society, and life that people care deeply about. The cash management service incorporates understanding of larger user trends and business missions. The legal strategy sees the long-term consequences for the client. The analysis of climate change policy arrives at consequences for price development. And the architectural prospect is integrated into a story about the function that the building will have in the surrounding landscape and in the context of larger cultural-historical tales. To accomplish this you need to zoom out. Zooming out is more than a trick to switch attention. Zooming out requires deep knowledge of the whole, and sometimes an eye for comparison. But let us start, once more, with a story.

HELICOPTERS, ROSES, AND THE SMELL OF OIL IN THE MORNING

"Oh my God! It is the same. We are in exactly the same lake, the same environment!" It was a beautiful morning in Luanda, Angola, in April 2009, and Ana Serrano Oñate was shouting and jumping with excitement. She and her team had been looking at pictures of rock samples from an old well, together with people from Sonangol, the state-owned company that oversees petroleum and natural gas production in Angola. To her surprise, Ana recognized characteristic rock structures resembling helicopters and roses in the pictures. She had seen these structures before in another Portuguese-language territory: Brazil. She was making the final connection between geologies on opposite sides of the Atlantic and across a time span of some 112 million years.

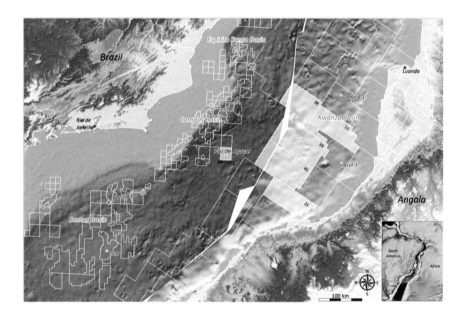

Ana is a fiery Spanish geologist in mid-career, known for her candid enthusiasm, spontaneous hugging, and her impatience when she is bringing ideas towards the finish line. Ana has run her own small geological company and worked for other oil companies. She is thoroughly familiar with the varied geology of Spain, Africa, the Middle East, and Brazil and has a well-developed ability for seeing connections. The Angolan eureka-moment was far from hers alone, however. It was part of a long chain of events during which people in Statoil, along with other oil companies, had recognized that South America and West Africa once belonged to the same continent. Parts of what we think of today as Brazil and Angola were connected 112 million years ago (see the illustrating image on the left). Consequently, discoveries and breakthroughs in understanding made on either side may have its counterpart on the other side of the Atlantic. So, when a series of surprising new discoveries were made in the deep layers below the salt sediments in the waters outside Brazil in the years prior to 2008, a rush to find parallels in Angola started. Were there pre-salt treasures there? Ana's visit to Angola in 2009 was part of a pre-salt collaborative effort across the Atlantic to find out.

What was special about the new discoveries on the Brazilian side was that they revealed a unique and new type of high-quality reservoir rock, a so-called microbial carbonate with travertine-like texture (the texture looks like the rock that ancient Rome was built from) that had never before been found to carry oil. If this kind of rock were to be found in Angola, it would mean a potential for huge discoveries – tens of billions of barrels of oil. What Ana saw that morning in Luanda was the exact same unique and rare type of rock that she had seen in a PhD report on the Brazilian discoveries, the very same travertine-like texture. It was the same lake, the same environment – the same treasure pot?

Three months later Ana was put in charge of the Paloma project and set out, in collaboration with Sonangol, to explore the size potential of the supposed reservoirs in Angola. She was given the assignment to acquire access to them. The Paloma project was organized according to geological accounts of earth formation 112 million years ago, and comprised a multidisciplinary group of people combining experience from Brazil and Angola. Said Ana:

"We compared the same quality seismic from both margins, types of structures and seals and also basin modelling – basically working out the lake as one, despite it now being split between Brazil and Angola."

It was a task force that worked in utter secrecy and with the passionate urgency of being first to make the very big catch. Less than a year after the April morning revelation, the team delivered and convinced exploration management to make a big bet. Finally, at the end of 2011, Statoil had gained access to five blocks of a total of 31,000 km^2, two with operating rights, in what many geologists hold to be potentially the most prosperous areas of the world. It remains to be seen what comes of it in the end, but that is not the point here. The point is the quality of zooming out in idea work.

IDEAS IN A PUZZLE

The story Ana was part of is mirrored by the words of Vidar Larsen, also a geologist who has participated in many successful exploration efforts. "Exploration operates within basic physical laws and is about putting together data in a large puzzle, basically knowing your field and doing long-term, science-based knowledge accumulation", he tells us, at first a bit sceptical about creativity and oil exploration having anything to do with each other. To Vidar, creativity seems the realm of self-indulgent artists, craftspeople and basket-weavers – people who, in his regard, are not as serious as scientists. By contrast, his work is extremely serious. He soon opens up, however, and he talks passionately about the importance of seeing the big picture in small-scale prospect analysis, about seeing regional wholes, not only singular blocks or licenses or prospects or wells, about being able to imagine geological processes that took place hundreds of millions of years ago, about the importance of conjuring alternative interpretations of the same data, about tectonic movements, thinking in four dimensions, seeing opportunities rather than problems, the use of sketches for zooming out, and the eternal need for persistence and passion in exploration.

"We don't find oil by looking at a computer screen, it's not that simple, it's not good enough. It's not about burying yourself in details; you have to understand the processes behind the details. We need to integrate so many observations. Geology is like a puzzle where you need to get a grasp of the totality very early. An image one can use is that of a tablecloth that someone is pulling by its sides. The cloth will have folds in different places, and it's about understanding how the whole cloth is moving. Then it can be useful to get help from someone who has data from another place, only remotely linked to your data. Perhaps they have a piece of the puzzle that you don't have access to and that can shed new light on your interpretation. The point is to see the big picture the entire time, but with a focus on where there is oil to be found. The danger is that one is stuck in one's box without understanding the big picture. We need to see the movement in the cloth."

Zooming out for both Ana and Vidar is about seeing large movements in the geology, daring to take one step back to get this full picture, zoom in again on the prospects and then acting swiftly on the consequences.

PARTS AND WHOLES

The importance of processes for zooming out stems from what we can call the circular and interpretive nature of all understanding, and thus also idea work: the never-ending dialectic between parts and their wholes (Palmer 1969, Klein and Myers 1999). Every idea of something is coloured by being placed in some larger and often implicit whole and vice versa – every whole is derived from its parts, which may also be implicit (Polanyi 1966). Thus, idea work switches between zooming in on particulars (the characteristic rock structures looking like helicopters and roses) and concrete ideas (that there could be a parallel discovery to Brazil) and zooming out on some larger coherent whole (the tectonic history of South America and Western Africa). To complicate things, there are many alternative wholes for every detail, and metaphors are a major device for being set on the pathways towards seeing new wholes. Unlike the puzzles we are used to, which have only one solution, geological observations can have many alternative explanations. And any idea or building can be placed in alternative stories, alternative landscapes.

IDEAS IN LANDSCAPES

Jenny, partner and landscape architect at Snøhetta, also mirrors the words of Ana. "Landscapes are what defines us as human beings", she says:

> "Your childhood landscape stays with you throughout your life – also the professional one – and this goes for non-architects as well. Everyone loves or hates places for these reasons: where you come from, the landscape you are born into, or the landscape you feel familiar with or the landscape you feel is a safe place, it's all something that affects us in how we draw. It decides what you like and dislike later in life, what ideas you approve of and which shapes you prefer. And I think that becomes accentuated in the processes where you go in one direction, where a concept actually can evolve so that you feel 'now, now it landed'. That feeling has a lot with identity and sense of place."

As a landscape architect, Jenny is not only an artist. She is also interested in the natural science disciplines, in chemistry, math, botany, and even in sociology. All these feed into her current work in an architectural practice. As she says:

"Architecture is almost always about creating something for the users, so of course you have to have the human perspective in it. And that extends to the human in relation to nature and landscape. I have always been very fond of the interface between art, culture, and the transition to design, and I found it very natural to be a landscape architect because I believe in seeing the larger picture – all the way to the city plan – and also the spaces between the buildings are what captivates me."

"Any project has a context that I will argue is always a landscape – if it is a city landscape, a field landscape, a moon land-scape, or if it's on the ocean. It is always, in the widest sense of the term, a landscape, and this, I think, is incredibly fascinating. It [a project] has to land on something; it has to be connected to something; it has to have coherence with something. So the in between, the leftovers, are *just* as important and to me most central."

In Norway, the places in between, stereotypically, are imagined as fjords, meadows, and mountains; in New York it is Central Park, the freeways, and Times Square that define these spaces. In these places, what happens constitutes the intersection between architecture, culture, and design. Contemporary architecture is a cross-border practice that traverses many aspects of our lives, society, and practice. But what about the landscape designers who make use of conceptual strategies to locate architectural practice? How are these two fields inspired and influenced by each other? Jenny has been working on Times Square. Times Square, New York, *a space between* illusions and realities, dreams and torments, a world where fame is pursued, magic staged, and very few people get to see their names in lights. Is this a contortion of what a landscape/space should be? Not to Jenny and the other landscape architects in the New York office of Snøhetta who are "changing the blanket while people are enjoying their picnic", as one of them eagerly exclaimed, standing there in the midst of chaos.

Landscapes, as our opening quote indicates, are carriers of larger socio-cultural histories. To the architects at Snøhetta and their clients, the culturally charged buildings placed in landscapes are successful in so far as they resonate with the larger stories of the land. The Alexandria library carries many references to the ancient pyramids and to the role of the Middle East as the cultural cradle of civilization. Signs from over 500 languages are carved into the surface stone. The Opera building in Oslo is designed to incorporate the social democratic notion of the "common land" – with a defining feature being a carpet-like open space available to the public free of charge. These are the references to foundational tales, stories of places that people live in, a context within and enveloping the design. Craig Dykers, partner and manager of Snøhetta's New York office, captures this sought-after quality of zooming out when talking about seeing the bigger picture in the "landscapes in the mind".

> "The places that we create allow for stories of the landscape to be projected into the landscape of the mind. I believe very powerfully in the nature of narrative. I think this distinguishes Snøhetta from a lot of other architecture companies."

IDEAS IN
STRATEGIES AND STORIES

Lawyers also zoom out. People at Thommessen, and their clients, frequently stress the importance of being able to switch between the particulars of a case and the larger strategic picture. What are the consequences for the client of alternative lines of action? Some projects stage such questions more clearly than others:

> "I was part of a DD [due diligence, the investigation or audit of a potential sale/investment of a company so as to carefully confirm all material facts and understand the totality of the transaction] where I was the one who put things together... That was so cool, because then you see the totality, and you are part of writing agreements and negotiations, and then you see that the findings you may have made have an effect on the agreement."

To the journalists at *A-magasinet*, zooming out comes with the air they all breathe. A key mark of a good story is that it enlists the readers in thinking about some larger societal and moral issue, whether it is how we see and take care of abused children, how we battle cancer, or how we live with wild animals. When writing a new article, journalists are expected to specify those larger themes that mundane stories imply and open up for.

To zoom out means being able to take a broader rather than a narrower perspective. To be a specialist involves a paradox: you must embed your knowing deeply, making your specialism an aperture though which a whole landscape can be zoomed with the resources of a deep, not shallow, framing, before finally focusing in on a detail, a fold, in the overall image. Great movie-makers understand this totally: Sergio Leone's epic film, *Once Upon a Time in the West*, concludes with a crane shot of Monument Valley, the favoured location for John Ford's westerns. The scene is a civilizing society building the railroad and its infrastructure for civic life. The characters who "once upon a time" populated the "wild" lawless west, meanwhile, are riding out of frame: they no longer belong there. As the camera slowly zooms in on the busy scene featuring railroad construction workers, it focuses on the progress of the only female character on the screen, Jill McBain, played by Claudia Cardinale. She is bringing a bucket of water to the thirsty crew. In this one scene, the prototypical masculine cowboy heroes of the story ride out of frame and a new, feminine figure moves into centre frame, with the camera picking up the folds of her dress, the detail of the water in the pail, underscoring that the story is entering a new fold: *Once Upon a Time in the West* has already passed into myth. All of this is represented, literally, by zooming out and slowly zooming in.

FOLDS AND LIGHTNESS

Big pictures, landscapes, embedded knowing, the fold, zoom, and focus – these are the metaphors that signify what we call zooming out. According to the philosopher Deleuze, the power and beauty of the fold is that a finite number of components can produce an infinite number of combinations. There is nothing "inside" or "outside" the fold – it folds in and out on itself. There are a variety of modalities of folds: the folding of time, or simply memory, the folding of the self on to its own conception of the selves it has been or could become. Listen to Dylan's "Brownsville Girl", a lyric that zooms in and out of specific detail and people and folds into a story about a story in which the most important thing is the loss of memory of detail. "Oh! If there's an original thought out there I could use it right now!"

In the masterful literary testament of the Italian author Italo Calvino, *Six Memos for the Next Millennium*, the first and perhaps most central chapter is about the relationship between weight and lightness. Calvino describes how much of his work is about removing weight – from people, details, seriousness, and existence – so that his stories gain a quality of lightness:

"Whenever humanity seems condemned to heaviness, I think I should fly like Perseus into a different space. I don't mean escaping into dreams or the irrational. I mean that I have to change my approach, look at the world from a different perspective, with a different logic and with fresh methods of cognition and verification." (Calvino 1985/1993: p. 7)

Calvino's mantra is perhaps the main clue to what is difficult but also life-enriching in zooming out. Extraordinary idea work consists in the discovery of new combinations, of new ways of folding the world into a new way of seeing – by holding details or prior understanding *lightly*, or letting them go. Much of the analytical apparatus that people in organizations use in their idea work is geared towards the weight of details and particulars. That is probably why a simple rule applies – when stuck or looking for a breakthrough, see the fold from a new angle – zoom out!

TIPS FOR PRACTICE

1. *Seek metaphorical lightness:* Facilitate emergence from immersion in data and rigorous analysis by playing with simplifying forms, metaphors and sketching. Do high-level comparisons with other concepts/ models. What class of models is your idea an example of or different from? Are there any analogies from other areas that could apply here?

2. *Seek physical lightness:* Facilitate movement away from details by shifting people's attention – take them away from the computer and out of the office to a river or a place with a view.

3. *Introduce zooming out moments* in meetings where you pause, step back, summarize and ask for the big picture.

4. *Conduct comprehensive mobilization strategies early* in large projects so that as many persons as possible participate in co-creating objectives, design, direction and work plans – it produces holistic understanding and flexibility in execution.

5. *Feed forward* by asking about potential consequences of the idea. What is the largest context in which this will have an effect? What does a future perfect situation look like if this idea succeeds?

6. *Cultivate "T-shaped" competence* profiles where people acquire a broad understanding of many specialized fields. Hire specialists with attitudes of openness and curiosity towards others' disciplines and specialties.

7. *Train newcomers to work with big picture issues* (e.g., regional work in exploration, strategy issues elsewhere) simultaneously or before they work on specific prospects.

THINGS TO AVOID

Never shifting attention or looking up from the computer or outside one's designated turf. Obsessing with details, being weighed down by them. Being stuck in confined spaces. Never letting people in on the whole process from beginning to end. Not having the knowledge required to see the big picture, whether in terms of strategy, history, culture, or contextual understanding. Believing that zooming out is a simple technicality that does not require deep knowledge of the whole.

RESOURCES FOR
LEARNING AND INSPIRATION

Basso, K. H. (1996). *Wisdom Sits in Places: Landscape and Language Among the Western Apache.* Albuquerque, NM: University of New Mexico Press. [An award-winning and profound book on how culture, history, and wisdom are inextricably intertwined with places and their landscapes.]

Calvino, I. (1985/1993). *Six Lessons for the Next Millennium.* New York, NY: Vintage International. [Calvino's literary testament is a series of lectures that was compiled and published by his wife after his death.]

Carlsen, A. and Mortensen, T. (2012). Against all odds? On the generative dialectics of imagination in exploration. Working paper. [The paper identifies and exemplifies how zooming out forms a key quality of exploration work, forming a dialectic pair with processes of immersing.]

Deleuze, G. (1993). *The Fold: Leibniz and the Baroque.* Minneapolis, MN: University of Minnesota Press. [The fold is a persistent Deleuzian metaphor; it allows Deleuze to muse on subjectivity, critiquing the presumption of a simple interiority and exteriority (appearance and essence, or surface and depth). Something folded announces that the inside is nothing more than a fold of the outside.]

Dylan, B. and Sheppard, S. (1986). "Brownsville Girl", on *Knocked Out, Loaded.* New York, NY: CBS Records. [A musical instance of a Deleuzian fold.]

Fawell, J. (2005). *The Art of Sergio Leone's Once Upon a Time in the West: A Critical Appreciation.* Jefferson, NC: McFarland. [One of the great films, critically and appreciatively examined.]

Isaacs, W. (1999). *Dialogue and the Art of Thinking Together.* New York, NY: Doubleday. [A practical and engaging book for joint inquiry in conversations, zooming out together. See the last chapter in particular: "Taking Wholeness Seriously".]

Klein, H. K. and Myers, M. D. (1999). A set of principles for conducting and evaluating interpretive field studies in information systems. *MIS Quarterly* 23(1): 67-94. [On the hermeneutics of interpretive field research. The article lists seven principles of interpretation, of which the most basic one is that all human understanding is achieved by iterating between considering the interdependent meaning of parts and the whole that they form.]

Leone, S. (1968). *One Upon a Time in the West.* Los Angeles, CA: Paramount Home Entertainment. [Where mythology met the brutal realism of the capitalism of the shifting frontier, populated by banditry, intimidation, capitalist resolve, property speculation, and iconic figures.]

Nicolini, D. (2009). Zooming in and out: Studying practices by switching lenses and trailing connections. *Organization Studies* 30 (12): 1391–1418. [A method paper explaining how to zoom in and out of different aspects of organizational practice. It works by switching theoretical lenses and re-positioning, so that certain aspects of the practice are fore-grounded.]

Palmer, R. E. (1969). *Hermeneutics*. Evanston, IL: Northwestern University Press. [An excellent text on the hermeneutical nature of all understanding, that people understand parts by understanding the wholes they form and vice versa.]

Polanyi, M. (1966). *The Tacit Dimension*. New York, NY: Doubleday & Co. [A classic text for explaining explicit and tacit knowing as focal and subsidiary awareness. Every act of knowing something new means zooming in on something that leaves other aspects of our knowing tacit.]

Smith, P. K. and Trope, Y. (2006). You focus on the forest when you're in charge of the trees: Power priming and abstract information processing. *Journal of Personality and Social Psychology*, 90(4), 578–596. [A good source to go to for understanding a cognitive psychology perspective on zooming out, how zooming out can be seen in relation to levels of abstraction and focus by which we attend to the world; being more principal, focusing on essentials and primaries, attending to patterns and structures, attending to goals beyond the here and now, feeling control.]

EXERCISES

1. What are the elements necessary for being able to zoom out in idea work? Which of these do you think is most difficult to bring about or master?

2. How long do you think it takes to zoom out: a minute, an hour, a month? Is it something you switch back and forth from by the second or a more elaborate process of dwelling – or perhaps sometimes both?

3. Who are the ultimate beneficiaries of your idea work? How do you think taking their perspective more fully and wholeheartedly could help your work?

4. Looking back at your own most successful idea work, when has zooming out been a part of it? What was decisive for managing to zoom out?

5. Looking ahead towards future idea work projects, how do you think the quality of zooming out could be better enabled? How would you do it in a project you are working on now?

6. Which other qualities of idea work do you think enable zooming out? How could getting physical help you zoom out? Or craving wonder? Or double rapid prototyping?

7. Do you see other concepts in organization theory that remind you of the quality of zooming out?

8. Describe an art experience that helped you zoom out.

CRAVING WONDER

WHY BURNING QUESTIONS OF A DIPMETER LOG, CARING FOR THE CLIENT, AND DWELLING ON THE 9/11 MEMORIAL GROUND HAVE THE SAME ORIGIN

ARNE CARLSEN, STEWART CLEGG, ARNE LINDSETH BYGDÅS[1]
AND REIDAR GJERSVIK

crav·ing won·der |
The sensuous experience of being in a mystery,
a combination of feeling startled and engaging
in passionate search. Wonder underpins all
imagination, empathy, and deep interest in
anything beyond self.

"Whoever is devoid of the capacity to wonder, whoever remains unmoved, whoever cannot contemplate or know the deep shudder of the soul in enchantment, might just as well be dead for he has already closed his eyes upon life"

Albert Einstein (in Koestler 1964/1989, p. 258)

"Do we always have to be only one? Why cannot I be Erle also? Why is the tongue always wet? What are really 'the old days'? What are the most oldest days? Who knows about them?"

Hannah, 4 years old

"He not busy being born is busy dying"

Bob Dylan (1965)

FROM A DIPMETER LOG AND A FEW HUNDRED MILLION BARRELS OF OIL...

One of the first persons we interviewed in the Idea Work project was Sigmund Hanslien, former Chief Geologist at Statoil and the protagonist behind the discovery of 700 million barrels of oil at the Grane Field in the North Sea in 1991. Sigmund is stout, professorial looking in an old-fashioned way, with rimmed glasses, and warm eyes but also with a manner that is a little challenging, implicitly suggesting, perhaps, that he might be thinking, "will this person be able to appreciate what I have to tell?"

Sigmund was working at Exxon during the events leading up to the Grane discovery. He was assigned to map an area where oil companies had been drilling wells for almost 20 years but with somewhat meager results. The only significant discovery was a field called Balder of 450 million barrels of oil, a field that Exxon had found in 1967. Sigmund started wondering about a well placed outside this field, to the north, where traces of oil also had been found. Could this oil be connected to the Balder discovery in the south? Such a prospect did not cohere with the model in existence for almost 20 years, a model that suggested the main oil discovery was contained in a structural trap.

> "I had these questions that just burned and burned: 'Darned, if this is a structural trap, why did not all the oil leak through the thin layers of sandstone that are above the main reservoir and that are also filled with oil? Is it possible that the oil instead is captured in a stratigraphic trap? Could the oil in the well far outside the structural closure be connected with the southern accumulation?' In that case, the extent of the discovery could be much larger than previously mapped. How could I convince management to spend hundreds of millions of kroner to investigate if this was the case?"

It was far from obvious that anyone would listen to Sigmund back then. After the Balder discovery, exploration in the region had up until this time provided disappointing results, and the oil industry was in a period with low prices and depressive moods. The key to moving ahead turned out to be the use of a dipmeter log from the well in question, a log usually used to measure the inclination of the beds in the subsurface. By using the dipmeter log in a new and creative way – to differentiate between oil- and water-bearing sandstones on a centimeter scale rather than a meter scale – Sigmund managed to demonstrate that the northern well had the same water-oil contact as the Balder discovery. Thus it was substantiated that both areas could be part of a common, large stratigraphic trap.

Traps are key models to understand where oil and gas could be contained in the underground. Simply stated, structural traps typically consist of isolated heights, often dome-like structures, with a top seal. Stratigraphic traps consist of pockets of hydrocarbon-bearing rocks surrounded by rocks that are impermeable for oil and gas, thus also with lateral and base seals. Identifying stratigraphic traps requires better geological understanding, and they are much more difficult to map than structural traps. Sigmund's questions were important because he raised doubt about the accepted model for trapping hydrocarbons over a large area with proven resources. Sigmund's colleagues describe him as a person who would pursue his deep-felt questions "even if 100 persons speak against him". Indeed, he did pursue his convictions, despite internal opposition and skeptical managers. He managed to persuade others to join him, first his colleague Morten Rye-Larsen, and was eventually allowed to acquire seismic data on the basis of his hypothesis. Voila! The prospect lit up clearly on the seismic. Sigmund's theory was confirmed and resulted in the Grane discovery. After these events, Sigmund's ideas were developed further by others, and they can also be seen as part of what led to the spectacular 2011 Sverdrup discovery to the south of Grane (see the chapter on Punk Production). Another company ended up exploiting Grane, but that's another story. About his approach to work, Sigmund says:

"I would just have to say that this is simply the way I work. It applies to both my hobbies and my work. I have this great desire to figure things out, to find answers. I *wonder* a lot. Whether it has to do with geology or not, the questions kind of take over, regardless of whether I ask others or try to figure it out for myself. My wife sometimes thinks it is too much. But I think wondering is a good thing in exploration."

Wonder is typically evoked by appreciation of some stimuli of beauty or strangeness, by feeling surprised, disturbed, unsettled, or amazed by something that triggers search, or, in Sigmund's words, "questions that burn and burn". With one of the fathers of modern philosophy, René Descartes, we may say that wonder is the first of all passions. With contemporary philosopher Martha Nussbaum (2001) we may see wonder as the basis for interest in anything beyond self and a precondition for empathy, compassion, and un-possessive love. Like a baby beginning to realize that there is a world to be explored, we all have the capacity to be taken by wonder when encountering the world and generating ideas of how it works. Wonder is decisive to cultivate imagination of absent pos-sibilities and absent others, the objects of wonder are those that people may care deeply about, and it is through wonder that children grow into their culture and people connect with worlds they do not know.

... TO CARING FOR THE CLIENT

"Barbie wins in the EFTA-Court" was the headline of a front-page story of the *Financial Times* one day in the early 90s. Siri Teigum, born in 1961 and a partner in Thommessen, is not particularly preoccupied with plastic dolls. But as an expert on EU/EEA law, she won a court a case for an entertainment television group broadcasting commercials directed at children. Siri is ranked as the best lawyer in competition law in Norway. To sit opposite her is reminiscent of being called on the carpet by a strict elementary school teacher whose eyes perceive any hint of mischief before it happens. She has bright blue eyes and a probing look that is exaggerated by large, oval lenses. Unabashedly, she says she is fully aware that many people think she's a bit scary. Hearing her say this, one might expect her to be reserved and distant but that is not the case. Siri comes across as open and generous, showing interest and curiosity in the person on the other side of the table. She is not a classic black-letter lawyer, deeply enmeshed in legal codes as objects of appreciation. No, her appreciation is very much turned towards the client. The clients and their projects form the major sources of mystery in her work.

"I think a lot about the clients. It came as a very big surprise to me. I thought that I was extremely interested in the law and would find it great fun to sit down and write about law. But it is even more fun to work with clients. They are very capable in their field and very dedicated to their projects, and I am stimulated in many ways by working with them. [...] There are almost no cases coming to us where the approach or the outcome is given. We are not that kind of firm. People come to us when cases are difficult in addition to being important. [...] The synthesis of questions, that is, to identify case elements and chief considerations and understand how they interrelate, that is of course what is the real challenge, and that means that you cannot say it's a simple puzzle."

Siri is a woman who speaks a great deal through metaphors. She likens her relationship as a lawyer to that of a doctor working with the parents of a sick child. The metaphor appears to be spot on. From the perspective of both clients and lawyers, "care for the client" is the most important quality of idea work at Thommessen.

"When a client comes to us with a case or a problem, it is comparable to going to the doctor and being worried that your children have become really sick. We really want to have someone solid as a rock who says: 'Now, follow me, I don't know what it is, but I'll go to this expert and then to that expert; I will gather all the threads and report to you regularly – or in the event of a special development – so you are always informed.' This is how we want things to be when we go somewhere with our children, and it's like that with clients too – they simply want someone who actually stands up for them and cares for the totality of their case, and thus for them. Sometimes the doctors say 'this disease is not something you will get rid of; you must live with it. It will be hard, but you can handle it.' Or they may say 'this disease will ultimately kill you, and you will die of this between six and 18 months from now. That's the way things are, but we will make it as easy for you as we can.' We do not want doctors to cry with us in such situations, or express themselves so that you may ask: 'Did you actually say I was going to die, or what was it that you said?' You have to be precise and honest when communicating with clients, particularly when you see that the outcome is uncertain and can be negative."

"I don't know what it is" – that is the key remark, because Siri can only work out what "it" is with the client. Care presupposes the ability to imagine the world of the client and a genuine, deep-seated interest in that world. It presupposes wonder. The clients and their cases are the mysteries to be carefully unraveled, stories capable of unfolding in many ways. For a lawyer of Siri's caliber, the client is a constant source of wonder. Such wonder is not soft or spiritual; it is deeply empirical and purposeful, in the way that John Dewey (1910, p. 31) saw wonder when he remarked that, "curiosity is the only sure guarantee of the acquisition of the primary facts upon which inference must base itself."

... TO DWELLING ON THE 9/11 MEMORIAL GROUND

The adult craving for wonder is strongest when we search for some higher principle, for what is good, true, and right. Arguing cases in the Supreme Court is an obvious way of connecting with such questions. Thinking about the ultimate purposes of architectural sites is another.

Craig Dykers, head of the Snøhetta New York office and one of the company's founders, was a member of the team that won a part of the commission for the redevelopment of the World Trade Center in the wake of the 9/11 terrorist attacks. Approaching this task is a difficult assignment for any architect. The site bears witness to the largest and most traumatic shock to the American collective consciousness since Pearl Harbor or even the Civil War. It is a haunted site, stalked not only by the spirits of those who lost there lives in the destruction but also by those whose lives were spared but shattered by trauma, loss, sickness, affinity, and a shared sense of violation. A scar on the city, it is nonetheless a scar that must be healed to make the city whole again, but healed in such a way that its sacred connotations are not lost in just another piece of real estate. As Craig sees the situation:

"The World Trade Center project is more than a sacred space. It is a major part of a world city, New York City. And not everybody sees death in the same way. Coming to terms with how you find the appropriate balance of creating a space that inspires an aspiration about the afterlife and about faith, while also creating a place where people can think about their everydayness, is the big balance. So I would say that we described the World Trade Center project as a place where you can go to remember and you can also go to forget. You have to be able to do both. The words strength, fortitude, resilience and hope, those are really positive things. I think we also need to bring out negative aspects of that site, like what are the manifestations of our society that allow for such a thing to happen."

"And so I'm hoping that our building, in the end, will be optimistic but not be absolutely seen as a marker for only goodness in life. It's not a very platonic form; it looks a little twisted and a little wrecked. But at the same time it's very pretty. Some people will probably just walk up to it and immediately see the reflections and the trees and see their face reflected in it, and think it's just a pretty gem. And other people will walk up to it and say: it's twisted, it looks like an airplane ran into it, you know. Nothing is, like, completely lined up, which is why it is so awkward. And those two things coexisting, will, I hope, make the building successful."

Across these three examples we see that wonder is marked by the twin qualities of enchantment and bewilderment, being in a dangerous romance. The wonderer as a person often appears to be somewhat restless, even anxious. Wonder is something *craved* and sought rather than a luxury activity. It is not the icing on the cake, but rather the essence of the experience. It is a craving that engages particularly valuable knowledge – knowing that is tacit, somatic, and *esthetic*. Wonder is felt as a bodily engagement, not as mere mental contemplation.

Kjetil Østli, journalist at *A-magasinet*, when explaining how he came up with some of his most valuable ideas for new feature articles, says: "If I can feel it in a purely physical way, if there is mystique there – it's a mystery, there is something untold – then the reader will feel that something is untold." The hunch has some basis in empirical evidence. From an analysis of the most emailed articles in *The New York Times* drawn from a sample of 7,000 articles published over three months, sociologists Berger and Milkman (2012) concluded that the most power-ful predictor of an article being emailed was its awe-inspiring nature. Readers most wanted to share articles that provided a feeling of elevation and admiration in the face of something greater than the self.

The experience of wonder underpins extraordinary idea work in many ways. Architects talk about the importance of attention to beauty, seeing "pearls in the sand", noticing what "feels right", and pursuing "bare-naked honesty" in discus-sions. Bankers talk about openness to ideas, impulses and needs of others, and "daring to be in a state of not knowing". Lawyers highlight, as we have seen, the ability to "genuinely care for the client" and imagine consequences of choices and strategies in their world. The founders of Point Carbon emphasize the generation of fundamental new questions as a prerequisite for keeping ideas flowing and anticipating new challenges. Exploration geologists express a deep reverence for nature and the exhilarating joy of finding out how the natural world works. Across all these examples, we might say that enchanted and powerful idea work begins in wonder, proceeds by means of a series of moments of wonder, and ends with an explanation that produces, when first seen or experienced, yet another new and powerful experience of wonder.

IS THIS YOU? WHAT IS THIS?

Artist and writer Rose Montgomery-Whicher (2002) has written a wise essay on how her engagement with drawing involves a visually embodied attentiveness to the world and seeing things anew. Drawing – or sketching – becomes a corporeal and relational activity that also works as a tool for renewing her wonder of places, things, and people. When taking a picture of her sister on a bench in the park in front of a wall of yellow roses, Montgomery-Whicher (2002: p. 43) describes the experience of seizing her in the moment: "I've caught you". Drawing her sister on a long train ride is a very different experience. Drawing makes Rose wonder how her sister came to be, who she is, what she thinks. It is an experience of letting the embodied mind ask a lingering metaphysical question: "Is this you?"

The sense of wonder echoes down the ages, through works such as Blake's (1833) *Auguries of Innocence*, with its opening stanza:

"To see a World in a Grain of Sand
And a Heaven in a Wild Flower
Hold Infinity in the palm of your hand
And Eternity in an hour"

The stanza, with its echoes of the Bible, still resonates in contemporary times in Dylan (1981):

"I can see the Master's hand
In every leaf that trembles
In every grain of sand"

If we can keep this sense of wonder, this capacity to see anew the familiar and the close at hand, in all its potential, to see the spiritual in the small things of everyday working life, then we can use wonder to produce extraordinary ideas.

TIPS FOR PRACTICE

Wonder is probably the quality of extraordinary idea work that is the most difficult to institutionalize as an organizational practice. Wonder cannot be controlled at the level of one specific activity. One can, however, cultivate habits of working that heed sources of mystery in the everyday, cultivate openness and receptivity to the unusual, and thereby increase the chance that wonder will happen:

1. *Look for oddities, things that do not fit, and the unusual* in order to train your senses of observation and appreciation of stimulus for wonder in everyday work.

2. *Expand the search by* allowing stimulus to be followed by free play of thought; tolerate uncertainty, bewilderment, and ambiguity; resist reaching for premature conclusions.

3. *Share the source of wonder* by telling others about that which startles and by engaging in long conversations of co-dwelling and co-discovery: "Look what I found! What could this mean?"

4. *Heed fundamental questions* that bear upon eternity, whether they are about the natural world or social matters of morality, truth, and justice.

5. *Uphold the indubitable mystery of colleagues and beneficiaries* of your work. Others can be the cradles of new ideas that cannot be arrived at if we categorize and stereotype them and their ideas in advance. Others should not be known a priori but imagined in such a way that presupposes their uniqueness and indetermination.

6. *Immersion*: Let go of self and seek imaginative participation in the phenomenon of investigation, getting on the inside, taking the eye of the other.

7. *Listen to your body*: Learn to appreciate the feeling of being startled that may instigate search and feeling of wholeness and beauty associated with breakthrough explanations and ideas.

THINGS TO AVOID

Denial. Regarding all explanations and solutions as final and considering wonder as an unnecessary activity that belongs in the realm of artists, scientists, and clergymen. Savoring blank astonishment that does not pass from admiration into searching. Disregarding embodied hunches and being suspicious of signs of passion in oneself or colleagues. Believing you have reached the truth or that some glimpse of truth is available *only* to your organization. Jumping restlessly from one puzzle to another and never allowing oneself to stay and dwell in inquiry. Overdoing it by never returning from wonder to action.

RESOURCES FOR
LEARNING AND INSPIRATION

Berger, J. and Milkman, J. L. (2012). What makes online content viral? *Journal of Marketing Research* 49(2) 192–205. [An analysis of which *New York Times* articles in a three-month periode that are likely to be emailed to others. Content that evokes high-arousal positive (awe) or negative (anger or anxiety) emotions is more viral.]

Blake, W. (1833). "Auguries of Inno-cence", in Keynes, G. (1969) *Blake: Complete Writings*. Oxford: Oxford University Press. [Blake's famous celebration of wonder.]

Carlsen, A. and Sandelands, L. (Forth-coming 2013). First passion: Towards a theory of wonder in organizational inquiry. Paper under editorial review. [Compares wonder in qualitative inquiry with instances of wonder in idea work and identifies four distinct moments of wonder that work together; stimulus, expansion, immersion, and explanation.]

Carlsen, A. and Dutton, J. (Eds) (2011). *Research Alive. Exploring Generative Moments in Doing Qualitative Re-search*. Copenhagen: Copenhagen Business School Press. [Calls atten-tion to wonder as a central feature in 40 personal tales of doing qualitative research.]

Carson, R. (1965/1998). *The Sense of Wonder*. New York, NY: Harper-Collins Publishers. [A beautiful treatment of the role of wonder in our relationship to nature, and how we can stimulate a sense of wonder in our children.]

Dewey, J. (1910). *How We Think*. Lex-ington, MA: D.C. Heath. [One of the books in which Dewey treats wonder in inquiry. For a related and more profound treatment that is more indirect on the topic of wonder, see his *Art as Experience.*]

Dylan, B. (1965). "It's alright, Ma, I'm only bleeding", on *Bringing It All Back Home*. New York, NY: CBS. [An exposition of many sources of won-der from a perspective that sees it as "life, and life only".]

Dylan, B. (1981). "Every Grain of Sand", on *Shot of Love*. New York, NY: CBS. [A more contemporary version of Blake's "Auguries of Innocence" celebrating a sense of wonder at the greatness present in the smallest of things.]

Heidegger, M. (1937–38/1994). *Basic Questions of Philosophy*. R. Rojcewicz and A. Schuwer (Trans.). Blooming-ton, IN: Indiana University Press. [A core text on Heidegger's treatment of wonder, one which distinguishes wonder from shallow curiosity and explains it as a way by which funda-mental questions of being come to people.]

Montgomery-Whicher, R. (2002). Drawing to attention. In M. van Manen (Ed.), *Writing in the Dark*. Ontario: Althouse, pp. 27–47. [Qualified in the text.]

Nussbaum, M. (2001). *Upheavals of Thought. The Intelligence of Emotions*. Cambridge, UK: Cambridge University Press. [A book not primarily on wonder but just the same efficient in describing how wonder is ingrained in human psychology, something that is not the exclusive realm of philosophers, scientists, or artists but that resides within all of us.]

Parsons, H. L. (1969). A philosophy of wonder. *Philosophy and Phenomenological Research* 30(1): 84–101. [A short and brilliant philosophical treatment of wonder, particularly good at explaining how wonder is a form of wound where people are being wonder-struck, stabbed awake with that which they do not understand.]

Platt, P. G. (1997). *Reason Diminished: Shakespeare & the Marvelous*. UK: University of Nebraska Press. [A historical treament of the role of wonder in literature with particular emphasis on the work of Shakespeare.]

Plato. (360 BC). Theaetetus. M. J. Leverett (trans.), M. Burnyeat (rev.). In J. M. Cooper (Ed.), *Plato. Complete Works*. Indianapolis, IN: Hacket Publishing Company, pp. 157–234. [The source of the oft-cited statement that philosophy begins and ends in wonder, taken from Socrates's dialogue with his student, Theaetetus.]

Rubinstein, M. (2008). *Strange Wonder: The Closure of Metaphysics and the Opening of Awe*. New York, NY: Columbia University Press. [This book is probably the best and most thorough contemporary intellectual treatment on wonder, comparing the treament of wonder in the philosophy of Martin Heidegger, Levinas, Nancy and Derrida.]

TED Conference 2011: *The Rediscovery of Wonder*. http://conferences.ted.com/TED2011/ [The TED conferece in 2011 was dedicated to the topic of wonder spanning a broad range of speakers from the worlds of art and science as well as the discovery and imagination of entrepreneurship. See also http://bitly.com/bundles/brainpicker/2.]

Shakespeare, W. *The Tempest*. Full script available at http://www.william-shakespeare.info/script-text-the-tempest.htm, accessed 17.02.2012 [*The Tempest* is Shakespeare's late masterpiece and one in which the nature of wonder is deeply explored. It recently inspired the Isles of Wonder theme at the 2012 opening ceremony of the Olympics, directed by Danny Boyle. *Tempest* is also the title of Dylan's latest work, although he denies any connection.]

EXERCISES

1. What are the key elements that go into the experience of wonder?

2. When do you think there could be too much wonder in idea work?
    Or too little?

3. Think about your experiences at work the last six months. When were
    you startled by something unexpected, strange, and/or beautiful?

4. What would you do to stimulate wonder in a particular project
    of idea work?

5. Which mysteries do you think are the most important ones for people
    in your organization to wonder about?

6. Can you think of instances when wonder was the driver of extra-
    ordinary idea work in your organization? What did it look like and
    what triggered it?

7. Looking across to other qualities of idea work: In light of the story of
    the artist drawing her sister, how do you suppose wonder is related to
    getting physical? What role could wonder have in double rapid proto-
    typing or in prepping? In activating which types of drama do you think
    wonder is particularly important?

8. What other concepts related to wonder explain what goes on
    in organizations?

ACTIVATING DRAMA

WHAT'S AT STAKE?

ARNE CARLSEN, STEWART CLEGG,
TORD F. MORTENSEN[1] AND REIDAR GJERSVIK

ac·ti·vat·ing dra·ma |
Calling people to adventure – into Battles, Mysteries,
Missions, Cathedral building, Treasure Hunts or the needs
of the human Other – in ways that recruit their utmost
capabilities and desires, asking: "Why do we come to
work here? What is really at stake?"

"The answer to your query as to what people go to seek in that country and why they fare thither through such great perils is to be sought in man's three-fold nature. One motive is fame and rivalry, for it is in the nature of man to seek places where great dangers may be met, and thus to win fame. A second motive is curiosity, for it is also in man's nature to wish to see and experience the things that he has heard about, and thus to learn whether the facts are as told or not. The third is desire for gain; for men seek wealth wherever they have heard that gain is to be gotten, though, on the other hand, there may be great dangers, too."

The King's Mirror, ca. 1250. Translated from Old Norse by Laurence Marcellus Larson, 1917

BUILDING CATHEDRALS

Faring thither through great perils: *Why* do we work with ideas? Why are some forms of idea work charged with more significance and engagement than others? For some projects, it is fairly obvious to anyone that the idea work going on is more than a regular nine-to-five job. The design and building of the new Alexandria library or the new Norwegian Opera building in Oslo or the 9/11 Memorial Museum in New York are all such examples. These are buildings and sites in which considerable political and institutional prestige has been invested, landmarks charged with enormous symbolic and cultural significance. These are projects that all redefine and enliven city spaces, the results of which allow people to celebrate the cultural significance of knowledge, to experience great art or to commemorate, mourn, and heal from atrocities. Few works of art, are used as much by people in their everyday life. And few projects leave their mark on their creators to the same degree. For many, participating in the creation of the Alexandria Library, Opera, or the 9/11 Memorial Museum are projects of a lifetime, experiences that will stay with them forever, that define who they are and what they leave behind. More than merely laying bricks, they have been building modern cathedrals. As such, these projects of architectural idea work speak to a set of answers to a larger set of questions that we can take from *The King's Mirror*: Why do we fare thither through such great perils when we work with ideas?

For drama we fare. Which dramas, and how are they activated?

FINDING TREASURES

Idea work is experienced as particularly meaningful when something is at stake, when the ideas people pursue connect with one or more forms of human drama. The things we consider to be at stake determine which ideas and projects to pursue, why people consider them important, and how they become deeply engaged. What is at stake greatly determines whether idea work is extraordinary or not. And what is at stake is sometimes dormant, unable to be seen or sensed. It needs to be activated.

Take the case of Peter Kahn, at present a highly respected geoscientist at Statoil's Houston office. He is also an accomplished poet and short story writer in his spare time, as well as the vice-chairman of AAPG (American Association of Petroleum Geoscientists). Peter is the kind of idea worker many turn to when they want a combination of broad knowledge and candid views. He offers seasoned, no-nonsense opinions, sometimes delivered with jovial, barking laughter, but always with respect for the receiver. When asked to recount a formative experience that shaped him as an explorer, Peter recalled an event in the early 1980s that occurred just after he had graduated from university and started to work in industry. At the time, Peter was still unsure of which particular career path he should pursue. A future in academia seemed alluring, for example. What happened during one week changed that ambition. Said Peter:

"I was assigned to follow up on the drilling on this fairly remote well-site up in the Rocky Mountains, about 170 miles from Salt Lake City. It was the week between Christmas and New Year's Eve and the job fell upon me since I was the most junior geologist there. It was just me and a couple of well engineers at the site. When we got to the point of drilling through our targeted prospect, there was no sign of oil. But there were indications from the log that the reservoir might be located a little deeper than we had thought. So after I reinterpreted the seismic and the log data, there was this decision point as to whether we should drill deeper or take our losses. It was my call. I said go ahead. On New Year's Eve, oil came to the pits! We had hit the jack-pot. All thoughts of entering academia just evaporated instantly: I had found what I wanted to do."

Peter's experience describes an event where he was called to the adventure of finding oil and gas. This is idea work, not in the service of building cathedrals, but as a modern treasure hunt where the various regional overviews, well logs, and seismic interpretations are the equivalents of treasure maps. Ideas about where to explore for hydrocarbons may result in finding grand treasures that bring wealth and fame. In Peter's case, the discovery was a solid 160 million barrels of oil, and there were bonuses to be reaped. But monetary gain is not the only attraction for Peter:

"What I realized is that exploration is such an adventure. It is hard to explain why some people relish this adventure and others do not. That is part of the mystery of what motivates people. For me, there is the sense of being the first explorer, and that *you* can accomplish this. Then there is the combination of going into the unknown with a certain set of tools and being absorbed by the possibilities of discovery."

People are called to the adventures of idea work in various ways. For some, the attraction may be to participate in a peak event where the stakes are particularly clear and they are privileged to be players. For others, it is seeing colleagues succeed. But the strongest recruiting mechanism seems to be participation in a challenging experience and mastering it, as Peter did. And this is not a vicarious experience or one where he plays a minor role. He makes the decisive call. Without his actions, the discovery might never have been made. He is the protagonist.

Several of Peter's colleagues describe a similar threshold experience that changed their entire orientation, a change from no longer "coming to work to analyze data" to thinking more holistically, being concerned with driving projects all the way and heeding the desire to find oil: "You just get hooked on it – there is this craving that you need to satisfy. The only comparable experience I have heard or read about is Jack London's rendering of the gold rush."

WINNING BATTLES

Or take the case of an annual highlight for the trading analysts at Point Carbon: in the first week of April every year, at a set time, the EU Commission publishes the carbon emission data for the previous year. Data from over 12,000 installations are released, and it is the only time of the year that the market is told the correct numbers for the previous year. For the analysts at Point Carbon and in competing firms, it is a major chance to calibrate the price models. The key is being able to turn around fast, show correspondence with one's own analysis, recalibrate one's models, and be the first to provide forward-looking market information that traders can use. A team leader of the carbon market portfolio explains:

> "It is like Christmas Eve and Constitution Day at the same time in the market. We work closely with our IT people to download all the databases fast, get them into the spread sheets, and then produce the correct answers to the price forecasting models. There is a lot of checking and thorough work going into this. When you get to this point, it's down-to-the-minute in terms of being ahead of the competitors. It's like [gesturing like a general to his troops] 'You – do the downloading! You – get it into the sheets! You – go update the

web! You – send the first PDF out!' And then we hold a web meeting with our clients two hours later. It's 'war room'-ish. Last year there were seven of us in this room, set up with extra wiring, food being brought in, you really see the teamwork. There are two things in this race, being first and being most correct in terms of our own previous forecasts. Last year our models were 0.2 % away from the actual data, by far the best in the market."

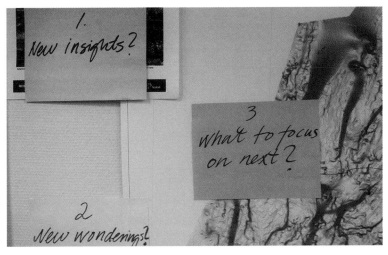

TYPES OF DRAMAS
AND THEIR COMBINATION

Ideas are more than vehicles of competitive advantage and economic gain. Ideas form part of how we create ourselves, how we form individual and collective identities. Working with ideas and the projects they fall into satisfies deeply held human needs of living with purpose, excitement, and hope. To a large extent, we are what we do and we live organizational life to the fullest when we experience participation in some type of positive drama, in adventures where something important is at stake and where we can make a difference. Such dramas come in many shapes. While architectural work ultimately may be seen as building modern cathedrals, the main drama of exploring for oil and gas has more to do with participating in treasure hunts and mysteries of the natural world. Winning a competition or making a discovery are company-making and definitive experiences, events people can tell heroic stories about and dine out on. Dramas give rise to the narrative capital that forms our identities. Our dramas define us.

Activating drama plays a key role in promoting engagement and drive in idea work. The table below presents types of dramas found in organizations and associated mechanisms for their activation (Carlsen 2008). It is not an exhaustive list but rather an indication of the variations in what is at stake when we fare thither. Activating drama may take place in many combinations across these themes.

Types of dramas	What is at stake	How it is activated
The Battle	To compete, to dominate and win	By identification of worthy enemies and battles/competitions
The Mission	To do good, to convert nonbelievers	By identification of worthy causes and uniqueness in ideology
The Mystery	To solve puzzles and explore new disciplinary/scientific ground	By identification of worthy puzzles or mystery
The Other	To enable positive personal development in other individuals	By assigned role and/or by identification of needing individuals
The Treasure Hunt	To find and seize valuable resources	By identification of resource prospects (and/or needs)
The Cathedral	To design/build constructions of great symbolical and historical significance	A combination of impact, newsworthiness, technological challenges, and lasting legacy

Going back to Point Carbon, the extraordinary drive in idea work and associated business development in this organization may indeed be seen as stemming from the activation of a powerful organizational drama. As voiced by one analyst:

> "What you really shouldn't underestimate is that in many companies people work there [because] they have to have a job, right? Most of the people who are in the carbon team work here because they have this sort of passion. [...] It brings us together."

This drama may be seen as having at least three components:

a) *Engaging in battles* with large established players. As expressed by one of the founders of the firm: "We are going to be 'Bloomberg with analytics', with a much better user interface, achieve world dominance ... there is absolutely no doubt in my mind that we can do it."

b) Emphasizing the joy of *exploring mysteries*; solving puzzles, following the need to understand and discover and the love of inquiring into complex issues. As expressed by a senior analyst: "I have this huge need to understand, to see things no-one has seen before." When such exploration results in unique knowledge, an intensely satisfying peak experience results: "nobody else in the world knows this, now I do, that's quite cool."

c) Taking part in a larger *pro-environmental Mission*. This is the most often mentioned motivational drive, in interviews as well as in interactions, exemplified by statements such as "we are contributing to making the Kyoto market transparent" and "when the EU Commission uses our analysis to make a [climate] policy, it's just a huge kick."

Several analysts at Point Carbon saw these elements of the organizational drama as coming together in a rush of adrenalin at the annual climate change conference in Copenhagen: "It's just the enormous pride in seeing the conference opened by Per-Otto [founder, then CEO]." The significance of the event may be seen as stemming from its being a peak moment within the inspiring project aimed at gaining market dominance and legitimacy for Point Carbon within a larger quest to reduce carbon emissions and contribute to environmental sustainability.

FRAMING EXPERIENCE AND CLARIFYING STAKES

In general, dramatic intensity in idea work varies with how much is at stake, the perceived risk and unpredictability, the importance of one's role, and the degree of exposure of the persons involved. Thus, to talk in terms of business law, dramas are more readily activated in cases argued in the Supreme Court, where fundamental questions of new law are at stake, or in major mergers and acquisitions that may decide the future of whole industries, than in mere routine cases. Likewise, dramas are more intense if the outcome is highly unpredictable rather than seemingly certain, and dramas are more intense if it is a case with considerable media exposure.

While acknowledging these more general patterns, it is important also to recognize that what is considered an important drama is a subjective matter that is open to interpretation and to influence. People may find intense dramas in things others consider trivial. One esteemed business lawyer cited a case pertaining to a boat docking space he was trying to win for a person he knew well. The case was particularly satisfying to the lawyer, because "it mattered a lot to him, and I know from my own experience how incredibly annoying such things can be". The same lawyer also tells of a case against a child molester, where the question of detention was stranded in technicalities. An internal sparring session produced the strategy that turned out to be decisive. By aptly wording the ultimate unacceptable consequence of the opponent's argument (in this case, that of the defense), the case was reframed and turned in favor of the prosecution: "What will you say to that when he rapes the next little girl?"

A similar example can be taken from the idea work of a building contractor. When a disagreement arose about the technical requirements for handicapped persons, the project leader brought a handicapped teenager in a wheelchair to the meeting: "I never saw anything like it – it totally changed the interaction, all disagreements about formal requirements were instantly forgotten about".

Another way of activating drama in idea work is through establishing milestones – drill schedules in exploration, deadlines in journalism and architectural competitions, the start of trials in legal work, and release of emission data for Point Carbon, as we have seen. Milestones are important motivational drivers because they expose teams to external attention, accentuate what is at stake and heighten the overall intensity of the experience. In the absence of milestones, simply giving teams continual internal attention may also count. As expressed by a junior explorer: "We are incredibly geared up when many people outside the team pay attention and are interested, when you feel you are part of something important, and there is a lot at stake."

At other times, the framing of experience as drama is subtler. There is an Italian fable that recounts an old peasant, on his deathbed, summoning his two feckless sons to hear his last words. Breathlessly, he proffers them advice. His final guiding word is that there is treasure buried in the fields that have been neglected since he fell ill and that it is for the taking. The two sons bury their father and then they start digging, digging, and digging. They find no buried treasure. They have, however, turned the soil, killed many of the weeds, and unintentionally prepared the ground for planting. The words of the old peasant activated several forms of drama. First of all, the lust for treasure, as well as the competition between the two sons, drives their digging – a competitive search. If these sons are fools, they will feel cheated when they realize that there is no treasure where they expected to find it. If they are wise, however, they will realize that their father has not cheated them but has instead given them the means and the motivation for unlocking the treasures of the field. The answer to their quest, literally, lies in the soil.

Sometimes we don't get what we want, but the search may provide us with what we need. All we have to do is activate the drama that can drive the search. In all these cases, bringing to the fore what is ultimately at stake, frames idea work and charges it with meaning and energy. *Why* do we work on these ideas?

INTO THE FIRE – WITHOUT SAFETY NETS

All cultural arts, of course, are filled with human dramas. One example of particular relevance here: in the epic crime movie *Godfather* by Francis Ford Coppola, one of the key scenes follows from a second attempt to kill the mafia boss Don Vito Corleone (Marlon Brando) by his rival, drug lord Sollozzo, and the corrupt chief police Captain McCluskey. Michael Corleone (Al Pacino), up until this juncture, has figured as the Americanized son who refused to take an active part in the "family business". Upon saving his father from the murder attempt and having his jaw broken by McCluskey, Michael, to his brothers' disbelief, offers to set up a talk with Sollozzo and McCluskey, during which he kills them both. The scenes mark Michael's entry into the drama, the moment when he is called to adventure (to defend his father), and the threshold experience where he irrevocably leaves his old life behind and starts on the path toward becoming the new godfather. The scene and the movie also become a threshold experience for Al Pacino as an actor and served to further escalate Coppola to fame.

Musical artists also know how to activate drama. The classic case is Miles Davis' *Kind of Blue*, where he took the band into the studio without charts and without rehearsal and just had them improvise over a rhythmic foundation. Most critics rate it as one of the best jazz albums ever – because of the way it sparks creativity between the players. Even more orthodox musicians, not from the jazz world, get this point about activating drama: when Dylan plays live he never ever plays the same set nor in the same way as he did the night before; both the set and the style will change – and the band members watch him like a hawk to follow his lead. Dylan activates drama by keeping the band and the audience permanently on edge – "what is this song? It's barely recognizable", are typical responses. These are dramas of existential creativity with no safety nets.

TIPS FOR PRACTICE

1. *Go for the big thrills at the edge of your capabilities*: Target the most challenging adventures of idea work (the toughest battles, the most valuable treasures, the most demanding mysteries, and the most worthy missions) that you think (your part of) the organization can successfully face. You can only thrive on the edge by seeking stretch goals.

2. *Seek higher purposes*: Tie your idea work in the organization to larger causes and struggles outside it: What larger societal and human purpose can your work possibly contribute to and how? Which of the ideas you work on have the potential to contribute the most to outside ideal causes?

3. *Invite and enroll* people in challenging, risky, and meaningful adventures of idea work, by allowing inexperienced persons to have significant roles, sharing peak moments, facing dangers together, and letting as many as possible take part in experiencing even small wins.

4. *Emphasize sources of pride* in the past. Ask your colleagues what they are most proud of in their previous idea work and former ideas. How can that pride be accentuated? What is the ultimate legacy from your ideas that you want to leave behind?

5. *Bring in end users*: Most people are driven by pro-social motives of wanting to make a difference. There are few reminders of ultimate purposes of one's idea work as effective as having end users tell personal stories about how they benefitted from your work and your ideas. Physical meetings with users are superior but videotaped testimonies and even images of end users are surprisingly effective in boosting moral and performance (Grant 2011).

6. *Charge projects and idea development efforts* by staging participatory launch events, enacting milestones and pressure, organizing benign internal competitions, and visualizing progress towards demanding goals.

7. *Ask the questions*: What are we *really* doing? *Why* do we come to work each day? What is the *meaning* of the ideas we bring to life? What are we most passionate about in our idea work? To what degree do we act according to these purposes and passions?

8. *Take stock of your own engagement*: If you have interest and enthusiasm for closely participating in the larger stakes of the organization's idea work, show it! If you don't, start thinking about doing something else.

THINGS TO AVOID

Coming to work to lay bricks rather than build cathedrals. Not taking responsibility for the results or caring about taking ideas all the way to the market. Indifference to what is at stake or particulars of work. Resting on one's laurels. Distancing oneself from the risk. Disengagement and its cousins: boredom, stagnation, and indifference. Overdoing it: dramas can also be entrapping and negative – too intense, unethical, not grounded in practice or with no balancing laughter.

RESOURCES FOR
LEARNING AND INSPIRATION

Amabile, T. and Kramer, S. (2011). *The Progress Principle: Using Small Wins to Ignite Joy, Engagement and Creativity at Work*. Boston, MA: Harvard Business School Press. [A recent practitioner oriented text that speaks to the significance of activating drama through small wins – how small wins within larger quests are pursued, noted, and communicated.]

Carlsen, A. (2008). Positive dramas. Enacting self-adventures in organizations. *Journal of Positive Psychology* 3(1): 55-75. [A comparative study on the types of dramas found in oil exploration, communication work, ICT consulting, and a vocational school.]

Crites, S. (1971). The narrative quality of experience. *Journal of the American Academy of Religion* 39: 291-311. [This is a seminal paper and a beautiful, profound text explaining how people make sense of their lives in and through stories in times past, present, and future.]

Grant, A. M. (2011). How customers can rally your troops: End users can energize your workforce far better than your managers can. *Harvard Business Review*, June: 97-103. [Adam Grant has, with colleagues, produced a fabulous line of research that explains how and why making a difference to beneficiaries of one's work is such a strong motivational force – in this context particularly telling of how to activate the drama of The Other. This article is a popularized summary of studies that can be accessed at www.management. wharton.upenn.edu/grant/]

Mattingly, C. F. (1998). *Healing Dramas and Clinical Plots: The Narrative Structure of Experience*. Cambridge, UK: Cambridge University Press. [An award-winning book on the storied nature of experience as exemplified in the healing dramas of occupational therapists and their patients.]

McAdams, D.P. (1993). *The Stories We Live By*. New York, NY: William Morrow. [On how and why people live their lives by stories, by a leading figure within narrative psychology.]

Roberts, L.M., Dutton, J.E., Spreitzer, G., Heaphy, E. and Quinn, R.E. (2005). Composing the reflected best self-portrait. Building pathways for becoming extra-ordinary in organizations. *Academy of Management Review*, 30 (4): 712-736. [This path-breaking article proposes a theory for how "jolts in experience" may set people on the pathway for becoming extraordinary, a parallel to how treshold experiences call people to adventure.]

Scheibe, K. E. (2000). *The Drama of Everyday Life*. Boston, MA: Harvard University Press. [This is an entertaining and well-written book by a narrative psychologist who takes drama as a primary frame for understanding a wide range of human experiencing, including eating, sex, and gambling.]

Vogler, C. (1998). *The Writer's Journey: Mythic Structure for Storytellers and Screenwriters*. London: Pan Books. [Vogler is masterful in pointing to structures of drama and ways of activating drama in movie screenwriting, particularly useful in terms of conceptualizing the notion of threshold experiences.]

Movies: *The Godfather* [For reasons explained above.]. *Million Dollar Baby* [For an example of the powerful forward-looking stories that shape people's lives and how such dramas provide hope for the future.] *Arven* [Danish]/*The Heritage* [For an example of how retrospective stories shapes people's lives, and how such dramas may be entrapping and lead to despair.]

EXERCISES

1. What do you think are the primary sources of engagement for people in your organization today? Which stories are implied in this engagement?

2. Look at the table with the six different types of dramas: Which of these stakes and ways of activating drama is particularly relevant for work in your organization today?

3. What do you see as the most important threshold experience in your work or your life as a student? When does mastering something represent the entry into a new frame, a new drama?

4. Which legacies are potentially produced in what you do – what could you leave behind?

5. Which truly exciting challenges would be exactly on the edge of the knowledge, skills, and capabilities of yourself and others in your organization?

6. Discuss the phrase "the more drama the better".

7. The Ancient Greeks divided drama into tragedy and comedy, and we have indicated that dramas may have serious ethical consequences. In this regard, when are dramas positive and when are they negative?

8. Dramas require staging: What are the essential props that you require to stage and activate inspiring organizational drama? What props can you drop? For example, think of the way Steve Jobs used to stage Apple product launches or Richard Branson launches new products; what makes such staging of organizational drama effective, for whom?

9. Think of two organizational dramas that you have been involved in, one great, one awful. Analyze the differences.

DARING TO IMAGINE

HOW GREAT IDEAS RESULT FROM CUTTING INTO THE ROCK, CELEBRATING YOUR DUSTERS, AND CHEERLEADING

ARNE CARLSEN, REIDAR GJERSVIK AND STEWART CLEGG

dar·ing to i·mag·ine|
Boldly venturing forth into unknown territory through creating shared imaginings, cultivating a language of possibility, handling failure, and providing encouragement.

"The question is not whether one will encounter obstacles; that obstacles will be encountered is a fact. The question is whether the creative leader has the fortitude to persevere. [...] Those who do not have the courage of their convictions may be many things – they will not be creative."

Robert Sternberg (2005: pp. 231–235)

The Peter Dass Museum at Alstadhaug in Northern Norway is cut into the rock behind the church where the Norwegian poet and pastor Petter Dass served at the end of the 17th century. The museum building, designed by Snøhetta, has received much attention for its integration with and respect for the historical site and the landscape, as well as for its bold and expressive architecture. The solution celebrated today was far from self-evident at the outset. When Snøhetta was commissioned to do the project, it had been planned at an entirely different site:

"The client did have a site that had been regulated for the purpose for twenty years. We did two different sketching projects for that site, but couldn't really get it. Then, instead, we cut the building into the rock, at the back of the church, to let the agricultural landscape – the entire landscape – and the existing buildings play first violin. And as you walked along a winding path, when you had seen everything else, then the building would open up. This was *totally* different. We changed the site. We were far beyond where we ought to be. We needed to regulate the whole area again. Various authorities needed to be involved, there were a lot of things to be done. And we thought: 'My god, they are never going to go along with this.' But when they saw it, they said: 'We have *got* to have this!' This is a super concrete example of a building that gives a totally different atmosphere and a much better tailored design to the site."

Jenny, partner and Senior Architect at Snøhetta, suggests that The
Petter Dass Museum is an example of a well-known occurrence in design
processes at Snøhetta: a total reframing of the project, disregarding given
constraints, and imagining and realizing new opportunities. This reframing, or re-imagination, happens despite the risk that it might jeopardize the
project, because the architects are so passionate about achieving the best
possible result and are convinced that the change will be well worth the
effort. Says Jenny:

> "I use to say: Don't give people what they think they want, because
> they deserve so much better! We, everybody, deserve so much bet-
> ter, and that includes the customer himself. Sometimes, they think
> they want this and that and the other thing, and you know what?
> – I say: 'If you know exactly what you want, you can get someone
> else to design that for you. Then you don't need Snøhetta.' It is
> this thing about the element of surprise – to put something into a
> different context, or combine it with other elements. It takes a lot
> to design something entirely new."

BREAK ON THROUGH

To change the entire basis of a project, even at the risk of failure, requires that someone manages to open up new spaces of possibilities and dares to pursue them against all odds. An important role of senior architects and partners in Snøhetta, including Jenny, is to bolster belief in new and different solutions, even when only dimly perceived. As one of the architects says:

> "One of the main drivers of creativity is that we have owners who aim to create unique architecture. That is reflected throughout the whole organization. One is willing to risk a lot to reach those aims, for better or for worse. It is an intuitive signal to those who work here that one is willing to do a lot to achieve these things."

Kjetil Trædal Thorsen is also a partner and one of the founders of Snøhetta. Although Snøhetta puts strong emphasis on the firm as a team, there is no doubt that Kjetil is a strong creative driving force. He has earned respect, not only in Snøhetta but among many architects in Norway and abroad, for his theoretical and philosophical insights and for Snøhetta's projects. In any of Snøhetta's projects, Kjetil has the ability to make the team strive for new, different and even impossible designs. Beyond his contributions to the design, Kjetil inspires others to go beyond previous achievements, to reframe assignments and open up new opportunities. As voiced by one architect:

> "It's all right that there is someone here to help you believe and dare to challenge the boundaries of the discipline. Even though I think everyone is equal in a team, I believe it is important that someone has the ability to give you this sense of self-confidence. Such belief and trust is contagious."

Today Kjetil dares to imagine from a position as a celebrated architect in an organization that supports it fully. Others have to dare when hope wanes.

"IT IS NOT ENOUGH THAT WE ARE THE ONLY ONES WHO SEE IT"

On a spring morning in 2008, Ketil Sollid, heading the regional team for the Barents Sea, in Statoil's Harstad offices, had to strengthen himself. He was about to once again ask the corporate exploration management committee for more funds to buy the new 3D seismic data from WesternGeco for an area in the Barents Sea. Since 1989, the area in question had been evaluated several times, the common perception being that hydrocarbons were there, but not enough to pursue. Attention to the area resurfaced in a prospect, Skrugard, during 2004–2005 when the regional team identified it as promising. The prospect was evaluated and proposed as part of the 19th concession round application. However, the area did not survive the internal ranking of prospects to be further investigated and drilled. Other prospects were chosen, prospects that looked unusually good and carried high expectations for large reservoirs of oil. The drilling of these prospects was a massive disappointment, yielding only non-commercial amounts of low-saturation gas and adding to a long string of dry wells in the Barents Sea. Many lost faith in the entire area. Furthermore, based on the 2D seismic survey, most people looking at the Skrugard prospect at that time would intuitively hold that it also probably contained only small pockets of gas. When the work on nominations for the 20th concession round started, the Skrugard prospect was re-investigated by the regional team and again, was proposed to be part of the nomination. But the area had no new information that could move the ideas forward. The haze of previous setbacks weighed heavily on people. Investing attention and reputation in another potential gas letdown? No chance. So, Skrugard again lost out in the internal nomination competition.

Despite all these setbacks, Ketil and others had never given up on the area's potential. They knew that the richness of opportunities in that part of the Barents Sea surpassed the time given to investigate them. Beneath the corporate radar, a small project was moved to the Bergen office so as to maintain attention. The fact that a 3D seismic survey was in the process of being shot indicated that others were optimistic as well. After finishing a re-evaluation of the area, Ketil found it hard to ask for funding. A close colleague, Jan Ove Hansen, gave him the final push:

> "We simply cannot risk not being in on this; we do not have the evidence for turning the area down. You've got to ask them."

So Ketil tried once more. This time, the management committee agreed to the purchase of 3D seismic data. Interpretation of the data commenced, with several companies in parallel trying to make sense from them. Who would be first to interpret the data and get access if the assessment they made indicated a discovery?

At Statoil, the Bergen group of explorers interpreted the new data. The decisive next step came when, in record time, geophysicist Audun Groth qualified and illustrated the existence of a so-called double flat-spot, indicating two layers of hydrocarbons. The image shown on the next page was a breakthrough device because it helped illustrate the core of the interpretation in a way that convinced the management team of the overall potential. "Audun has a real gift in trimming the data so that the essence becomes part of a convincing story", Ketil explained. It was also crucial that this story could be backed by solid analysis that had already been done of the flat spots of all the wells in the area. Thus, when the internal quality assessors asked tough questions, Ketil's team could answer without the kind of hesitation that might seed doubt. The rest, as they say, is history.

After the decision was made to reprioritize the prospect as number one, the company mobilized swiftly and with force to acquire the acreage, being able to draw upon a whole tradition of previous studies and analytic work to qualify the application. Statoil managed to win the rights for a new exploration license and drilled the prospect in early 2011. An oil find of some 260 million barrels (as estimated at the time of writing) was the result. Skrugard had become the "high-impact"-discovery everyone had hoped for. It was shortly followed by a comparable discovery in a neighbor prospect, Havis, one year later. Currently, companies that had abandoned the Barents Sea are moving back with renewed optimism for the now proven oil province. The change from that spring morning in 2008 could hardly have been greater.

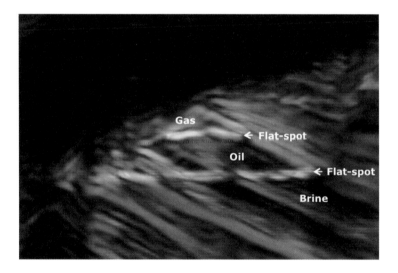

What lessons can be learned from the Skrugard case? One lesson is clearly that daring to imagine might mean persevering against all odds for many years, keeping hope and not giving up until the opportunity arises to prove one's ideas viable. Another, and perhaps even more profound insight, is that to come up with ideas that are later realized, the imagination needs to be relational, something one sees together with other people. Says Jan Ove Hansen:

"In retrospect one can always say that one time or another we have had ideas that correspond to all the prospects that are now proven. But these ideas are always subject to change – imaginings that weaken or grow depending on new information and that must survive tough competitions against other prospects. It is our responsibility to back our beliefs, mature our ideas. In the end you need to convince decision makers that the one you are championing is the best – our leaders also need to be able to imagine there is oil there and believe in it. It is not enough that we are the only ones who see it."

A LANGUAGE OF THE POSSIBLE

The biggest fear that the founders of Point Carbon have about the idea work of the firm is that the analysts will stop being able to anticipate future demand. They have successfully anticipated future demand several times, most significantly when anticipating the carbon market ahead of EU legislation. Five minutes after the announcement of the European Union Emission Trading Scheme on 12 October 2003, which opened the trading of emission credits/CO_2 quotas as of 1 January 2005, the analysts at Point Carbon published the first news bulletins on that new market. Will they be ahead of the game next time?

It is an understandable fear – what can be harder? Daring to imagine means actively looking for opportunities, going first where nobody has gone before, cultivating a language of possibility. One feature here is simply to have people scan for the new and install some way of sharing the fragments and glimpses of the future, whether market legislation, new technologies, or new patterns of demand. The apparatus behind news bulletins in trading analysis, or scout services in oil exploration, are examples of that.

Another key mechanism is a language rich in metaphors and analogies – "what if this is like...?" Metaphors are bridges between different specialties. As exemplified in the chapter on Liberating Laughter, playing with new terms and metaphors allowed analysts of Point Carbon to build bridges between domains and to define the market. Likewise, explorers talk about different *play models:* How and where has the oil been created? How and where has it been transported? And how and where has it been trapped and stored, making it possible to find and possibly be extracted? Depending on the play model, you will look for different geological and seismological cues. The repertoire of play models is a repertoire of possibilities.

A third feature of the language of possibilities is simply questions. Lawyers at Thommessen emphasize the importance of daring to "be ragingly stupid, dare ask those elementary idiot questions so that we understand this well enough". The clients of the firm second this, even to the point of showing openly what one is uncertain about: "someone being able to hold and express different kinds of opinions between them, and that's very good; that's a strength. It shows that there are several possibilities." The road to imagining new solutions goes through new questions.

Finally, a language of possibilities means a focus on opportunities rather than only on problems and constraints. In many cases, oil explorers in Statoil are looking for oil in the same places that hundreds of explorers have searched before, including close colleagues. In these cases, it is necessary to have the faith to assume that previous work is incomplete. One can do this by focusing both on what works and on what does not work. As one explorer stated:

> "There are many ways to present things. One can put forward a message by looking more at the possibilities, less at the risks. You need to find a balance here. I think it is key to look at possibilities, not impossibilities. It's the easiest thing in the world to break down prospects. It's hard to build them up again."

CELEBRATING DUSTERS

When oil wells deliver disappointing results, they are "dry": without exploitable amounts of oil and gas. Particularly dry wells are called "dusters". A duster is a well without traces of hydrocarbons and is a clear failure, even if it may provide valuable new geological information. Magnar Larsen at the Statoil Harstad office was part of a team that received the Duster of the Year Award in 1990, a year before he and his team found 500 million barrels of oil in the Norne discovery.

We can only speculate about the connection between the duster and the Norne discovery. What we can say is that celebrating dusters is a way of handling failure that rewards efforts rather than output, crucial for idea work in any high-risk environment. Reflecting upon his most rewarding work experiences as an explorer, another geologist expressed it as follows:

> "Well, you know what, the most exciting story I have been part of is probably a dry hole. You always feel bad when it turns out like that, because you had so much hope that it was going to work, especially when it's kind of your baby. But the executive manager of exploration was very gracious. He said: 'The worst thing about that play was that we don't have ten more just like it'."

Snøhetta has a way of handling failures that parallels this story. In the winner-takes-all settings of architectural competitions, the firm wins about one in 10. Obviously, how the nine "failures" are handled can have dire consequences for what people learn in their idea work and what they dare imagine next. This explains why Snøhetta does not just do the obvious thing of celebrating successes (who would not?) but also celebrates the efforts made in the entries that did not win, recognizing the great things that fail to make the one in 10. It may also explain why a favourite quote of Ole Gustavsen, director and partner in Snøhetta, is from Winston Churchill: "Success is the ability to go from one failure to another with no loss of enthusiasm."

Daring to imagine presupposes the ability to treat not only successes but also failures as collective accomplishments and to learn from them.

CHEERLEADING

Prying open the new and handling failures are two sides of the same coin. Both are closely associated with courage. Courage comes from the same word as French "coeur", Latin "cor" = heart. In some sense it means to "follow your heart", meaning your passion, commitment, belief – idea! But it is a question not only of following your heart or idea, but also following it in spite of your fear of what might happen if you do so. In the words of Rollo May:

> "Courage is not a virtue or value among other personal values like love or fidelity. It is the foundation that underlies and gives reality to all other virtues and personal values. Without courage our love pales into mere dependency. Without courage our fidelity becomes conformism. In human beings courage is necessary to make *being* and *becoming* possible." May (1975: p. 13)

Courage might mean going beyond the program of an architectural competition, giving advice your client won't like, suggesting that several billion dollars be spent on drilling for oil and gas that might not be there, inviting outsiders to participate in something you don't have 100 per cent control of, promising to deliver something you haven't yet made and don't really know how to accomplish.

A related word, and also key to extraordinary idea work, is to *encourage*, meaning to "help someone gain courage". Ways to encourage in idea work span from building upon the understanding of others, to supporting people when things are difficult, to communicating recognition, or seeing the best in others. It is well summed up by a senior exploration leader who is renowned among many of the people working for him for his ability to bolster faith and confidence in others. How so? In his words:

"We've got uncertainty in risking [risk assess-
ments], in what we do, we've got uncertainty when
it comes to the license rounds. [...] So I mean, if
you don't have encouragement, it's hard to deal
with all that uncertainty. And my job, I feel, is to
walk around, show interest, sit down with them
and provide support... to be a cheerleader, first
of all that."

ALL THE WAY TO HIMALAYA

Beyond cheerleading and dusters and cutting into the rock, daring to imagine is not only about ideas of new products, services, or where oil can be found. It is also about daring to grasp and share the dreams of what one truly desires, what individuals and the organization as a whole can become. Without such daring, the founders of Snøhetta would never have entered the competition for the Alexandria library in the first place. And the founders of Point Carbon would never have pioneered the carbon market or thought they could be leaders in other forms of trading analytics.

When daring to imagine the new, you always begin somewhere, sometimes in a small act that points to what can be. At other times it is a commitment:

"Until one is committed, there is hesitancy, the chance to draw back, always ineffectiveness. Concerning all acts of initiative (and creation), there is one elementary truth, the ignorance of which kills countless ideas and splendid plans: that at the moment one definitely commits oneself, providence moves too. A whole stream of events issue from the decision, raising in one's favor all manner of unforeseen incidents, meetings and material assistance, which no man could have dreamed would have come his way. I learned a deep respect for one of Goethe's couplets: Whatever you can do or dream you can, begin it. Boldness has genius, power and magic in it!"

W. H. Murray (1951), *The Scottish Himalayan Expedition* [the couplet, while beautiful, is actually not from Goethe]

Boldly venturing forth into unknown territory by breaking new ground, cultivating a language of possibility, convincing others, handling failure, and providing encouragement, is the task of many artists as their style, repertoire, palette, and other devices evolve. Think of the many "periods" in Picasso's work, for instance. For artists whose work is performed in public, rather than painted in private, the challenges can be especially acute. There are the famous audience refusals that artists sometimes inspire: one of the most famous in history was the premiere of Stravinsky's *Rites of Spring* in Paris in 1913. It's innovative structure and melodies, signaling a decisive end to nineteenth century Romanticism, provoked a riot that started with catcalls and boos from the audience and broke out into fistfights, and which eventually led to the police intervening after the intermission to restore a semblance of order. A similar incident happened with Luigi Pirandello's now widely celebrated *Six Characters in Search of an Author,* perhaps the first postmodern play in the history of the theatre. At the premiere in Rome in 1921, the furious audience split up into supporters and adversaries, the latter shouting "Madhouse! Madhouse!" while Pirandello himself and his daughter escaped hurriedly through a side exit.

Likewise, as captured on the famous bootleg recording of the Free Trade Hall concert of 1966, Dylan also provokes boos, demonstratively slow handclapping and catcalls from an audience, not all of whom were prepared to follow him from the world of acoustic folk balladry to hard core blues and driving rock. "Judas!", was shouted from the hall: "I don't believe you. You're a liar, ... play it loud, ... play it fucking loud", retorted Dylan, at the beginning of an impassioned "Like A Rolling Stone". Sometimes, daring to imagine much more than an audience's presuppositions can point to the future both through producing something other than that expected and through the ways in which the adverse response to the shock of the new can encourage and stimulate further creativity. If the customer were always king, the arts would be a very dull place indeed. And the same goes for many other spheres of idea work.

TIPS FOR PRACTICE

1. *Go first*: The most basic tip for daring to imagine is as glaringly banal as it is difficult to follow. For the Petter Dass museum, the Skrugard prospect, and the Himalaya expedition, someone had to take the first committing step (going against the client, asking the management team again, deciding to launch the expedition) without any security net, leading the way so that others could follow.

2. *Build belief by rewarding efforts, not only outcomes:* Give attention to and celebrate original contributions, ambitions, and bold projects even when they do not produce great outcomes – for example through rituals like "duster of the year". A few critical experiences of how failure is handled in the organization can make a significant difference for how courageous people are.

3. *Scan, gather, and share clues:* Want to try something that is energizing, culture-building, and useful for organizations that cannot afford their own scout services? Arrange repeated two-hour sessions three to four times a year for sharing and discussing clues to the future – whether glimpses of new demand, technology, industry trends, or something else. Every participant brings at least one clue. Use simple visual reminders of selected clues on a web or a physical wall. For a practical way of setting it up, look at: *http://www.strategicbusinessinsights.com/scan/process.shtml*

4. *Make cheerleading a virtue*: Few things are more energizing than affirmative communication by which you actively express interest in others, look for the sparks of genius in them, and appreciate both results and seeds of what can be. Ways to this are numerous: cheerleading at presentations, project groups and individuals, organizing "cheerleader of the month" and "five kudos a day keeps gloom away", or positive announcements at meetings, etc.

5. *Share stories about what has worked in the past*, ranging from high-stake projects to the successful handling of threats and crises to smaller everyday events. Such sharing should not be limited to annual events. It can be done on a weekly basis. Success stories are particularly effective if they come directly from end users.

6. *Communicate with invitation and inquiry* (Dutton 2003): "What do you mean by that? What is really the basic problem/need here? How can we solve that?" – rather than an argumentative approach: "this is the solution because... I am right because..." Attend to wishes and needs rather than orders and specifications, solutions and future rather than problems and past.

7. *Show vulnerability* by being open about your own anxieties, fears, fragilities, and near-failures that turned out well. This is particularly important, for leaders and other role models who people look up to.

8. *Practice your pitch:* Daring to imagine means convincing others that what you have seen is possible and worthwhile doing. It is a sell that might need repeated rehearsal and preparation to answer tough objections.

9. *Protect the early stage of the creative process from critical scrutiny.* Pay attention to vulnerable clues and unfinished but potentially fruitful ideas by temporarily suspending doubt and developing them until they have enough backing to undergo critical scrutiny.

THINGS TO AVOID

Only dwelling on problems, barriers, and inadequacies. Giving up
before one has tried or tested one's understanding or because tangential
ideas have failed. Attaching failures to individuals. Discouraging others
through one-sided negative feedback, distrust, or problem-oriented talk.
Believing one cannot succeed where others have failed. Engaging in mere
daydreaming without acting upon one's hopes and desires. Failing to
enlist others in one's imagination and building their belief. Not making
the final commitment.

RESOURCES FOR
LEARNING AND INSPIRATION

Alexander, T. M. (1990). The pragmatic imagination. *Trans. Charles S. Peirce Society* 26(3): 325–348. [A profound academic text on the theoretical underpinnings of imagination from pragmatist philosophy, covering both how imagination is situated in the everyday and why it presupposes self-reliance and hope.]

Bandura, A. (1989). *Human Agency in Social Cognitive Theory.* Boston, MA: Harvard Business School Press. [A reference text on self-efficacy – people's belief in their capabilities to influence the quality of their functioning and reach important goals – from the originator of the term. Bandura is the most cited of all living psychologists and this is one of his key works.]

Carlsen, A., Hagen, A.L. and Mortensen, T.F. (2011). Imagining hope in organizations: From individual goal-attainment to horizons of relational possibility. In Cameron, K. and Spreitzer, G. (Eds.) *Handbook of Positive Organizational Scholarship.* (pp. 288–303). New York, NY: Oxford University Press. [The article goes through alternative theories of hope in organizations and links them to imagination.]

Dutton, J. E. (2003). *Energize Your Workplace: How to Create and Sustain High-Quality Connections at Work.* San Francisco, CA: Jossey-Bass. [This book provides a highly useful account on respectful engangement at work, particularly relevant here in terms of being genuine, showing vulnerability as well as communicating affirmation and support.]

Kearney, R. (1998). *Poetics of Imagining.* New York, NY: Fordham University Press. [An intellectual feast summarizing the contributions from continental philosophers to the topic of imagination.]

May, R. (1975). *The Courage to Create.* New York, NY: W.W. Norton & Co. [This book is a highly accessible and well written treatise on courage in creativity.]

Miller, H. (1997). Why don't you try to write? In Barron, F., Montuori, A. and Barron, A. (eds.) *Creators on Creating.* New York, NY: Jeremy P. Tarcher / Penguin. [A wonderful personal tale on daring to be receptive to one's creative impulses.]

Murphy, I. (2004). Imagination as joint activity: The case of architectural interaction. *Mind, Culture and Activity* 11(4): 267–278. [One of the few empirical articles about the practice of imagination at work.]

Murray, W. H. (1951). *The Scottish Himalaya Expedition.* London: J.M. Dent & Sons. [The book tells the story of the first Scottish expedition in 1950 to the Kumaon range in the Himalayas, between Tibet and western Nepal. The expedition, led by Murray, attempted nine mountains and climbed five, in over 450 miles of mountainous travel.]

Sternberg, R. (2005). WICS: A model of positive educational leadership comprising wisdom, intelligence, and creativity synthesized. *Educational Psychology Review* 17(3) 191–262. [An explanation of the WICS-model – wisdom, intelligence, creativity, synthesized – of educational leadership by one of the thought leaders in creativity research.]

Worline, M. (2011). Courage in organizations: An integrative view of the "difficult virtue". In Cameron, K. and Spreitzer, G. (Eds.) *Handbook of Positive Organizational Scholarship.* (pp. 304–315). New York, NY: Oxford University Press. [A fine, recent summary of the concept of courage in organizations.]

EXERCISES

1. List the key elements of daring to imagine. Which of them seems the most important?

2. Do you think that daring and imagination always belong together? Why/why not?

3. What is courage in your role as a student? In other organizational activities where idea work is central?

4. Have you worked in an organization that has a way to reward courageous efforts (such as, for instance, "Duster of the Year")? If yes, how does it work? Ask someone who has received the reward what she or he thought about it. If not, imagine what such a prize could be: What effort should be rewarded? What would the effect be on the people and teams that you know?

5. Looking back at your own most successful idea work – whether as a student or in another organizational setting – what characterized the most successful imagination of something new that you have been part of?

6. Looking ahead towards future efforts of idea work, again possibly including your thesis work as a student, what could you do in practice to be more boldly imaginative?

7. Looking across to other qualities of idea work: What are the ways that daring to imagine is helped by other qualities? Could daring be stifled by some of them? What, for example, is the relationship between daring to imagine and generative resistance?

8. Looking to theories of creativity, innovation, or knowledge creation: Do you think that the role of imagination and/or courage is well covered? Can you think of examples of contributions?

GETTING PHYSICAL

WHAT IS IT WITH THOSE SKETCHES – AND WHY ARE PIN-UPS MUST-HAVES IN IDEA WORK?

ARNE CARLSEN, STEWART CLEGG,
TORD F. MORTENSEN[1] AND REIDAR GJERSVIK

get·ting phys·i·cal |
Moving from over-dependence on electronic media and towards *materializing* and *visualizing* ideas in artifacts, *touching* ideas, *sketching* ideas, *gesticulating* around ideas, and *moving* while doing idea work.

"In most firms, there is social pressure to do everything and put everything on the computer. It is the gold standard for current 'best practices'. (p. 48) [...] at a certain point, the graphics are so spectacular, the sketches so precise, that possibilities can feel like inevitabilities. Detailed hand drawing once signalled that major design problems had been resolved, when computers produce such drawings, they cue a similar response. Today's designers may experience that sense of completion, even when they know it is not warranted. [...] In digital format, even preliminary ideas look finished."

Sherry Turkle (2009: pp. 48–57), *Simulation and its Discontents*

We are sitting in the office of Per-Otto Wold, one of the founders of Point Carbon, and at the time also the company's CEO. Per-Otto is a young athletic man, one who embodies the stereotype of the rugged Norseman, afraid-of-nothing, capable of conquering new worlds, a force of nature. We are interviewing him about the origin of the firm, an organization that pioneered trading analytics for the carbon market and quickly rose to dominance in segments of gas and power trade. As usual, Per-Otto displays a peculiar mixture of restlessness, reflexivity, and direct, almost blunt, speech. After meetings with him and one of his co-founders, Atle Christiansen, we sometimes find ourselves talking faster for hours, smitten by their energy. We are some five minutes into the conversation when Per-Otto gets up and walks over to his stylish office cabinet, taking out two large rolled-up sheets of paper from the upper drawer. They are slightly yellow and pale, almost as if they were old papyrus rolls. He proudly lays them out on the table: "Here you have the first Carbon Market Trader and Power Market Trader."

Oh, again – sketches! The sheets are sketches of web-based applications for trading analytics, applications that Point Carbon pioneered (see the image below). They are reminiscent of something we have seen in several other contexts: Idea workers in all industries seem to do a lot of sketching, sometimes with incredible passion. Indeed, behind most great ideas there seem to be a succession of sketches. What is it with sketches? Isn't their significance in idea work counterintuitive to the abundance of digital tools and personal computing?

1. Sketch of the first Carbon Market Trader application at Point Carbon

2. The first sketch of the idea of the Norne Discovery

3. Frank Gehry's sketch of the Tree House University of Technology, Sydney

1.

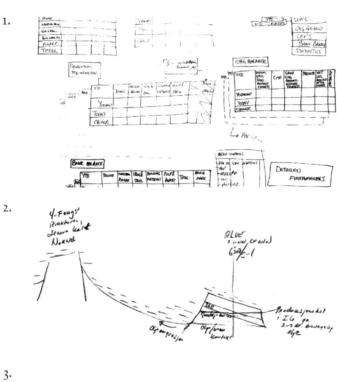

2.

3.

Getting physical with idea work invariably involves sketching. The first time we noticed the importance of sketches was during an interview with Magnar Larsen, a long timer at Statoil's northernmost exploration office in Harstad: "Making notes on paper, and scribbling, triggers processes in my brain." Indeed, a key ingredient in the story of the Norne discovery is that the decisive idea, after months of prep work and generative resistance to previous ideas, was conceived on a piece of paper in a coffee lounge.

We know of many other occasions such as this: Two friends sketching a 2x2 model on a beer mat that became a bestselling book in organization theory (Burrell and Morgan 1979). Frank Gehry sketching a tree house on a napkin as the inspiration for a new university building in Sydney (*http://www.dezeen.com/2010/12/17/dr-chau-chak-wing-building-by-frank-gehry/*). Gehry, in conversation with the dean, imagined the new building as a tree of knowledge, which quickly was represented as a tree house. The tree house was just a quick doodle on the back of a coaster. Nonetheless, it morphed into an organic, grounded, but slightly askew structure, rambling like a tree, and has since evolved in iterations of over 150 three-dimensional models. The initial quirky, jokey sketch has become a material object in the process of being built that is already hyped as Sydney's most significant building since the Opera House. From a simple sketch, enthusiasm and energy have been generated, prototypes modeled, decisions made, and an AU $160 million dollar budget signed.

Getting physical means getting your ideas into your hands together with your colleagues. Sketches are important because they transport idea work from the realm of individual contemplation to visual interaction and cocreation. With sketches, along with other artifacts, ideas become objects for joint attention and development. Because of this, sketches underpin many other drivers of extraordinary idea work. Sketches, for example, are ideal for shifting attention from details to larger wholes, thus enabling us to zoom out and clarify concepts. As noted by another explorer:

> "To generate an understanding, I draw simple sketches. Having difficulty drawing sketches amounts to difficulty in arriving at a proper understanding of the concept."

Sketches are also ideal for presenting half-worked ideas on the fly, allowing for the easiest form of prototyping there can be. In this sense, sketches counter the tendency of solitary workers to create output that looks more finished than it actually is because of its computerized and digital design. Lack of contact with the physical world in idea work can produce the equivalent of what some explorers refer to as "Nintendo Geology". These observations in the Idea Work project mirror those of MIT Professor Sherry Turkle as previewed in the opening quote.

More fundamentally, sketches comprise one of the clues to why extraordinary idea work must get physical. For Magnar, the importance of sketches falls within a larger recognition of the physical nature of exploration work:

> "I have it in my reflexes that I think well when I sit down and work with paper, like scribbling on the completion logs. Completion logs are some of the best products we have in exploration. Logs are made by people who have been hands-on at the well. They have been sitting next to the well, seen the sand with the oil shows and so forth, taken down all the information on the logs. You can bring up a log on the screen, but then you do not get all the interpretations people have of them. If you have it physically in front of you and take notes and scribble, it just sinks into your head... when you have PDF-reports 178 pages long on your screen and start scrolling, it's really slow. Books are simply much faster and you can take notes. [...] I am renowned for my messy office. Clean desk is not for me. I need my papers around me. I have many personal things on my shelves, material that dates back as far as the 80s. I pull it off the shelf when I need it, when I wonder about something that I know I have touched on before and need something concrete to go on. Then I remember an old report and pull it out. With these modern offices, that part of our creativity is lost."

Artists work in this way, as well. Bob Dylan, in *Chronicles Volume 1,* explained how his whole approach to song writing changed as a result of taking painting lessons from Norman Raeben. From these lessons he learned both a different perspective on narrative time, one that was non-linear, and the importance of stripped-down capture of the matter at hand. From learning and doing sketches, a new approach to songs emerged. Elsewhere, and earlier, in a *Playboy* interview in March 1966, Dylan talks about the physical roots of inspiration, checking the sounds that draw attention, that move the imagination, that touch the body, that help to create that thin, wild mercury sound:

> "That ethereal twilight light, you know. It's the sound of the street with the sunrays, the sun shining down at a particular time, on a particular type of building. A particular type of people walking on a particular type of street. It's an outdoor sound that drifts even into open windows that you can hear. The sound of bells and distant railroad trains and arguments in apartments and the clinking of silverware and knives and forks and beating with leather straps. It's all... it's all there. Just lack of a jackhammer, you know. Yeah, no jack-hammer sounds, no airplane sounds. All pretty natural sounds. It's water, you know water trickling down a brook. It's light flowing. Usually it's the crack of dawn. Music filters out to me in the crack of dawn."

Sounds, sketches, completion logs, books and reports from the shelf can all serve as media for physical interaction. Being able to scribble next to the results and ideas of others creates visual bridges to one's own thoughts and ideas.

HANDS - ON

Sketches are also significant because they allow for tactile engagement. It is a well-established insight in what is known as the tradition of "grounded cognition" (see for example Barsalou 2008) that what you do and the spatial and material context in which you find yourself when you learn about or think about something heavily influences your idea work. For instance, it has been shown that the sight of a graspable object will activate the same neurons responsible for actually grasping that object (Gallese 2003), and even more strikingly and relevant in the present setting, the metaphor of grasping a concept activates the same neurons (Wilson and Gibbs 2007).

The world is represented and processed through not only cognitive but also sensory-motor processes. One way this is seen is through gesturing. Indeed, peak moments in idea work, as described by people in the case organizations during sessions we have videotaped, seem to be curiously accompanied by increased, intense gesturing. When videotapes of interactions are fast-tracked, one can literally see gesturing increasing before and during peak moments. It is as if bodily involvement itself brings forward ideas as participants use their hands to emphasize points, open up, connect arguments, and make visual contours of tentative solutions. Tversky (2009, pp. 130–131) provides part of the explanation:

> "Gestures [...] are effective in part because their relationship to meaning is more direct, less mediated. In addition, and in contrast to words and diagrams, gestures can embody the knowledge they are meant to convey."

Thinking about an idea draws on the brain's capacity to imagine experiences – contexts, situations, bodily states, and feeling – that are associated with the idea. The term "grounded" refers to the different ways cognition is grounded in these different modalities and contexts and associated with how the body interacts with the physical world (Barsalou 2008).

Sometimes the very term, "thinking", in an everyday sense of the word, is insufficient for capturing what is actually going on. Patricia, an explorer at another Statoil office, explains:

"It's an immersion process – you sort of soak it up, and it becomes a very subliminal kind of almost passive thing, if you can let yourself go. Now, some people can't do that; they're too rigid. I'm an intuitive person by nature, but it's... you know, I solve more problems by looking at data over here, or somebody else's problem, you know. I'll solve my own problem, or it'll come to me, when I let my body relax. [...] I will still produce paper copy – and I'll get my colored pencils out, and I'll do that, because it is the way – it is a way – you really have to do the physical part sometimes. To get it into your head... to really get that extra dimension."

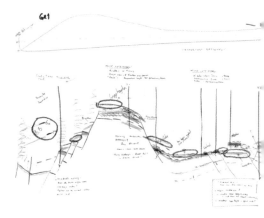

Patricia's account underlines the pioneering work of Mark Johnson (2007), who talks of breakthroughs in understanding as being *felt qualities* of a situation, bodily-felt hunches and anticipations that are later discriminated into what we call theory and concepts – or ideas. Still, Patricia's story describes solitary idea work aided by physical tools and embodied involvement. *Collective* work in co-creating ideas may also benefit from tapping into knowledge that is embodied. In general terms, getting physical – in a collective sense– often involves *materialization* of ideas in artifacts and interaction with them. Some fields of work are visual by nature. Oil exploration is an imagination-intensive form of work in which visuals of prospects where oil might be found are placed on various maps:

> "[There are] many big regional maps. We look at things and drink coffee in our corner, with big maps in front of us. And then not only people in our exploration team, but also people who work with business/field development, join in. So people who work on a field up here [pointing to map], they like to discuss what's happening down here [ditto]."

Wall displays are artifacts that may mediate idea work both within and between teams, and project spaces may be places to touch, sketch, dwell over, and wonder about, while seeing how things connect. Explorers' talk is filled with nostalgia about those projects where all team members interacted seamlessly in dedicated spaces. The contrary situation is considered to be individual work where people are trapped in front of a computer and send fragments of analysis back and forth in email relay races.

It might be no coincidence that in the most successful company in the world at the present time, Apple, one of Steve Jobs' allegedly strong dislikes was the use of slides to present ideas. In Walter Isaacson's recent biography on Steve Jobs, Apple's chief designer, Jonathan Ive, tells of a room in Apple's design studio where all prototypes are laid out for display, to be touched and played with. Ive explains how, when he was still in good health, Jobs used to come to the room every day to feel the products in his hands while discussing the future of the company: "Looking at the models on these tables, he can see the future for the next three years." (Isaacson 2011: p. 346). In no small way, idea work can be literally hands-on.

AND HERE COMES THE PIN-UP

At Snøhetta, other artifacts often accompany sketches, such as photos of the larger landscape, images of other buildings, symbolic images and drawings that communicate a concept and, of course, a series of small-scale models of buildings and sites. The architects at Snøhetta's New York office have combined the use of many such artifacts in a scheme the architects have coined pin-up. Every project has its own place on the wall, and the project's material is pinned up continually (such as printed 3D model drawings and reference pictures). Meetings, including those with clients, are held in front of these walls to facilitate decisions and to discuss the recent contributions of each project group member. The pin-up functions as the project group's collective memory, a chronology of the development of ideas and as a shared overview of the totality of ideas. At the start of subsequent sessions, the elements of the pin-up remind team members where they left off in previous discussions as help to focus attention on the issues at hand. When a project phase is concluded, all the drawings and diagrams are pulled down to make room for the next projects.

For anyone familiar with crime series and detective stories, Snøhetta's pin-ups strike a familiar chord. The wall becomes an accumulation of clues that enable continuity in discussions and stimulate advanced pattern recognition. Inspired by Snøhetta's pin-up scheme, we introduced a similar practice for a small and close-knit exploration team who were given the task of identifying four drilling prospects near a recent area where oil was discovered. The allotted time was less than half of what was usual. We arranged for a simple pin-up wall showing prospective drill sites on regional maps, with a variety of detailed information and sketches for each. All team meetings, including the final ranking, were held in front of this display, which was updated as work progressed. The experiment succeeded. The group delivered before schedule and above expectations.

Part of the success of pin-ups is that they rely on human faculties in understanding spatial information and making spatial inferences. We take these faculties for granted – they are expressed inherently in everyday language when people think about ideas spatially (Tversky 2009, p. 211.): "like *getting close to* someone, feeling *upbeat, arriving* at an insight, *entering* a new field, *wrapping* one's head *around* an idea". The interaction in front of the displays becomes embodied interaction around a variety of representations and objects that allow a simultaneous look at both details and the whole – an event that involves both moving and seeing together.

GETTING PHYSICAL
AT WORKSHOPS

What about other, less visual forms of work? At SpareBank 1, a key design feature of a series of successful idea workshops involving both technology suppliers and clients was to get physical using mockups (Garfinkel 1967) and other devices:

- *Movable idea cards:* Physical representation of input ideas on hard copy cards with associated images, each idea card drawn by one participant (who would have to champion it) and also represented on a large wall poster where all input ideas are shown

- *House of ideas:* Mapping of developed ideas on large 2x2-meter wall spaces organized as houses with separate idea rooms

- *On their feet, moving and marking:* the entire workshop is organized in front of walls and tables (without chairs), where people move about and stand in front of visuals they have co-created, marked/colored/scribbled on, and combined

We wrap up with a story from where we started, at Point Carbon. We are 12 hours into the 1½-day workshop to discuss the future portfolio of products and services in the carbon market. Suddenly there is a standstill. The intense discussion, analysis, and preparatory work have seemingly led to little more than a repetition and overview of previous thoughts. Is that all there is? The participants leave the building for a walk, continue talking, and then pick up where they left off, sketching, when they return. The pace increases, there is energy, and new metaphors emerge – new ideas *begin to flow!* We got physical.

TIPS FOR PRACTICE

1. *Get the gear:* Establish low threshold environments for producing and documenting ideas on the fly, at the speed of imagination. Have an abundance of sketchbooks, colored pens, boards, wall space, and sheets available everywhere.

2. *Sketch & build it:* Get your thinking into your hands together with your colleagues by using displays, diagrams, maps, brain maps, models, and artifacts to materialize hunches into drawings and other shared models.

3. *Pitch ideas unplugged:* Make sure that individuals and teams pitch presentations unplugged, repeatedly and early, in order to invite participation and to adjust the course before it's too late.

4. *Touch your "data":* Whenever you work on a difficult problem requiring coding or synthesizing input from many sources, try representing such input physically on movable objects, such as, for example, pieces of paper. Then start touching, coloring, marking, and moving this input around looking for new combinations.

5. *Pin it up:* Share work in progress by hanging it up on the wall for others to see. Institutionalize such sharing by designating walls, spaces or rooms for this purpose. Establish organizational routines for informal as well as formal interchanges in front of the pin-ups. Every large idea work project should have its pin-up.

6. *Scrap the clean desk policy:* Personalize desk space. Make room space group-centered. As far as practically possible, encourage local storage of books, reports, and any other artifacts that may be useful in creative discussions.

7. *Reclaim workspace design* as part of line management, not facility management. Start by i) having all idea workers photograph their favorite space for being creative and pinning all these on the wall, and ii) ask everyone to state one way in which the work space could better support their efforts. Protect sacred spaces and distinguish between places for i) deep and prolonged concentration, ii) intense interaction, iii) places for serendipitous encounters, iv) places for visualization of new ideas, and iv) informal talking and walking.

8. *Move!* Change your physical surroundings in accordance with the knowledge and purpose at hand, and be sure to use your body when doing idea work: walking, talking, sitting, standing, wandering, running, biking, golfing, etc.

THINGS TO AVOID

One solution fits all types of problems. Clean desk policy and depersonal-
ized workspaces. Meeting rooms without daylight and organized (only)
around monologues and PowerPoint communication. Lack of team space
or project space with ample room for joint sketching and pinning up
fragments of ideas. Only communicating by email or phone. Keeping files
of ideas in huge databases and not making them something you can reach
for, physically. Thinking of formal knowledge management systems as
the only way to share ideas with others. Disregarding bodily felt signs of
inspiration and intuition.

RESOURCES FOR
LEARNING AND INSPIRATION

Barsalou, L. W. (2008). Grounded cognition. *Annual Review of Psychology,* 59, 617–645. [A key source for the theoretical tradition of grounded cognition.]

Boje, D. (2012). *Quantum Storytelling: Black-smithing Art in the Quantum Age.* [In this video, presented at the 4th Process Symposium in Kos, Greece in June 2012, David Boje bridges the roles of organizational scholar and philosopher with a side career as an accomplished blacksmith – heavily inspired by the philosophy of Martin Heidegger.]

Burrell, G. and Morgan, G. (1979). *Sociological Paradigms and Organizatioal Analysis.* London: Heinemann. [Taking two debates in sociology, "order" versus "conflict" and "actor" versus "system" the authors sketched out a 2x2 table on the back of a beer mat in a favourite pub. This became the source of the paradigms model that was the main feature of the subsequent book. The ideas changed a little in their implementation but remain recognizable in terms of their genesis.]

DEGW. The Cabinet of Wonder, in BOX, London School of Economics. http://www.boxexchange.net [BOX is collaborative space supporting UK public sector at the London School of Economics. The Cabinet of Wonder is a cabinet/wall/shelf with an eclectic mix of objects that are seemingly meaningless, but it is supposed to enable the viewer to see the world in a multitude of different ways. By use of light, sounds, and real artifacts, the Cabinet is meant to encourage discussion and original thinking among individuals and teams.]

Doorley, S. and Witthoft. S. (2012). *Make Space. How to Set the Stage for Creative Collaboration.* Hoboken, NJ: John Wiley. [A fresh and novel book from Stanford University's design school on strategies for changing physical work space to enhance the ways in which teams and individuals collaborate and innovate.]

Dylan, B. (1966). *The Playboy Interview,* accessed 31.10.1. [The alleged recluse opens up and talks freely about many things – including the physicality of inspiration.]

Dylan, B. (2004). *Chronicles, Volume 1.* New York, NY: Simon & Schuster. [A biography of complex folds in which narrative assumptions of linearity are suspended.]

Ewenstein, B. and Whyte, J. (2009). Knowledge practices in design: The role of visual representations as "epistemic objects". *Organization Studies* 30 (1) 7-30. [An empirical study of the use of visual representations in architectural work that is also a useful intro to the large literature on boundary objects in organizations.]

Gallese V. (2003). A neuroscientific grasp of concepts: From control to representation. *Phil. Trans. Royal Soc. London,* B., 358: 1231–1240, 2003. [Research on the relationship between what we can see and touch, and our conceptual representations and internal world models.]

Garfinkel, H. (1967). *Studies in Ethnomethodology.* Englewood Cliffs, NJ: Prentice-Hall. [The classical tap-root of much of the later "practice"-oriented studies of management and organizations. Garfinkel shows how attention to detail in the small things of everyday life yields returns in seeing how order is sustained and complexity is managed.]

Isaacson, W. (2011). *Steve Jobs*. New York, NY: Simon & Schuster. [Recognized as the definitive biography.]

Johnson, M. (2007). *The Meaning of the Body: Aesthetics of Human Understanding.* Chicago, IL: Chicago University Press. [A pioneering work on the embodied, visceral basis for all understanding and meaning-making, drawing heavily on classical pragmatism, psychology of art, and neuroscience.]

Mortensen, T. (forthcoming 2013). *Unplugged Creativity.* Manuscript in preparation for doctoral dissertation. Department of Psychology. University of Oslo. [A study of creativity in oil exploration that emphasizes how its physical nature, including the pervasive use of low tech sketches, maps, scribbling on well logs, etc., co-exists with advanced technology for imaging and interpretation.]

Sibbet, D. (2010). *Visual Meetings: How Graphics, Sticky Notes & Idea Mapping Can Transform Productivity.* Hoboken, NJ: John Wiley. [A practitioner-oriented account on how to work with visuals in meetings, one of several by this author.]

Turkle, S. (2009). *Simulation and its Discontents.* Cambridge, MA: The MIT Press. [A book on the generational and technological divide between the "real world" of physical objects and tools and the "imagined or simulated worlds" introduced by technologies of simulation and visualization.]

Tversky, B. (2008). Spatial cognition: *Embodied and situated.* In P. Robbins and M. Aydede (eds.), *The Cambridge Handbook of Situated Cognition.* Cambridge, UK: Cambridge University Press, pp. 201–216. [A summation of much current understanding in the field of spatial cognition from one of the world's leading experts.]

Tversky, B., Heiser, J., Lee, P. and Daniel, M.P. (2009). Explanations in gesture, diagram, and word. In Coventry, K. R., Tenbrink, T. and Bateman, J. (eds.), *Spatial Language and Dialogue.* Oxford: Oxford University Press. [An article discussing the interplay between three modes of communication – through words, gestures, and diagrams.]

Wilson, N. and Gibbs, R. W., Jr. (2007). Real and imagined body movement primes metaphor comprehension. *Cognitive Science: A Multidisciplinary Journal* 31(4), 721–731. [Empirical research that supports the idea that appropriate body action, or even imagined action, enhances people's understanding of metaphorical concepts.]

EXERCISES

1. What are the key elements of getting physical in idea work? Why is getting physical important?

2. What does getting physical mean in your idea work? What are the things, the artifacts, that you and your co-workers share, talk about, and work with in meetings, in the office, or over a cup of coffee? Name three, ask your co-workers to do the same, and share your lists. What are they? How do you use them? Could you use them more effectively? Are there other artifacts that might promote your idea work?

3. How and where do you meet when interacting on ideas? Think about your last normal working week and set up a list of the various ways you worked together with others; where and how. How does this affect the results of your idea work in a positive or negative way?

4. Think about a project or task you have been a part of (at work, at university, in your community, or wherever), and that you regard as especially creative, productive, energizing, or positive in any way: Where did you work? Which physical tools did you use? How did you materialize your ideas?

5. When people in distant geographical places work together, it is hard to argue that they should meet in the same room and relate to the same physical artifacts. How can one "get physical" in such a setting?

6. How do you see the connection between getting physical and the other qualities of extraordinary idea work? Getting physical and prepping? And craving wonder? And zooming out?

7. Can you think of examples of idea work where getting physical might be counterproductive or of less importance?

8. Seen through the lens of getting physical, describe the key features of an ideal team space. How would it differ for different types of idea work?

9. Taking a broad look, which parts of social science do you think have most to teach us about getting physical in idea work?

DOUBLE RAPID PROTOTYPING

HOW MAGNUS LEARNED TO BEAT THE BIG FAT CATS AND WHY HE FEARS BECOMING ONE

ARNE CARLSEN, STEWART CLEGG AND REIDAR GJERSVIK

dou·ble rap·id pro·to·typ·ing|
A work form that seeks to force speedy production, testing, and improvement of half-worked ideas so that they are shared and bolstered at an early stage of development.

"Offer as many prototypes as possible within the limits of your budget and schedule. You'll avoid some awkward conversations. You'll get more honest genuine feedback. And you'll learn from each prototype so that the finished result can be smarter, better, and more successful than the prototypes that got you there."

Tom Kelley (2005: pp. 56), *The Ten Faces of Innovation*

CLOSE TO THE CLIENT

Prototypes? That sounds like a piece of metal made in a mechanical tool shop or a foam object in a design firm. What does that have to do with, for example, feature journalism or legal work?

Let's begin by eavesdropping. We hear the kind of conversation that might occur in any young, entrepreneurial organization making its mark in the world. In fact, this conversation took place in the sleek downtown offices of an innovative business situated in the emerging markets for climate change costing, tax, and reform. We first hear from the part of the firm that supports power trading.

"Our competitors, the established brokers – they were large, fat cats. They sat there with the heavy established models they had developed and did weekly updates that they faxed to everyone, long lists with numbers. That was their style; marketing letters and stuff that was always a bit late, more concerned with perfecting their large models, remote from the everyday hardcore traders."

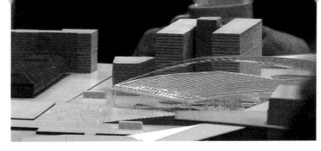

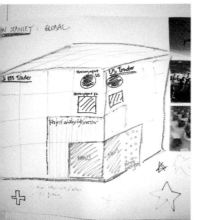

It is Magnus Køber who is speaking, and as he speaks his hands move fluently, and his gaze darts around the room. Magnus is the kind of person who seldom sits still during a conversation. With his penetrating gaze, unruly hair over a sometimes well-trimmed goatee, and casual look, Magnus is prone to jumping up for a quick sketch or to breaking out in spontaneous outbursts of enthusiasm and laughter. In his late 30s, Magnus describes himself as an impatient geek who is fond of machines and gadgets.

Magnus's energetic restlessness typifies in many ways a style of idea work that has been formative for the trade analysis company, Point Carbon; the company that, more than any other, pioneered the market function of trading CO_2-emission quotas and that is also a leader in supplying trading analytics to gas and power markets. Point Carbon's success is owed in no small measure to the habit of engaging clients in rapid co-production of new services and following a "launch-then-hire" strategy. Magnus came to Point Carbon after building up the analysis division of a power broking firm from four persons into a market leader. He is now director of Point Carbon's services for the power market

> "It's all about being close to the client. We were so physically close
> to the traders, so close that we had this constant feedback on what
> they wanted. We literally sat there and listened to their shouting
> and questions: 'How is it going? Are there any wet forecasts? What's
> up now with this producer or that one…?' You know, when there are
> wetter weather forecasts, that means more rain in the system and
> the entire supply-curve shifts, there is more power available. Then
> people turn around and many have to sell and some need to take a
> loss because they have gambled on there being less power, and so on.
> The essence is really very simple – is the price going up or down?"

"We realized that what the traders really need is fast updates on a continuous basis. So we optimized our system for that purpose, getting weather forecasts and other info fast and converting it to what it meant for supply and demand. We were fast on new technology. The web was still fairly new at the time, so the others were using faxes and stuff. So we were the first to build a web-based service for power traders. It was fast, looked good, supplied what the traders needed, and we instantly got a lot of clients. The development of the system was equally fast, responding to new types of questions by launching new menus and buttons in a day or two, and then putting it right out there again."

Magnus is a prototype prototyper – an innovative designer of innovative ways of doing things. His latest initiative is what he calls "hackathons": two-day sessions where web developers interact intensely, sometimes around the clock, fully concentrated on producing and testing new functionality of the trading analysis models on the web. All of these experiential trials are variants of what we call prototyping. Prototyping follows from the counter-intuitive insight that we must first act to make sense of what we are doing. To filch and switch a famous line that leading organizational theorist, Karl Weick, has repeatedly borrowed from one of the forefathers of creativity theory, Graham Wallas: "How can I know what I think until I see what I prototype?" In Magnus' case one might ask: "How do we know what to offer until we see what we can make and get some reactions?"

Prototyping can involve very simple, small experiments. Successful prototyping allows for repeated interaction across internal and external boundaries and results in proposals that are being judged as increasingly plausible and valuable as key sources of uncertainty are addressed from one trial to the next.

Magnus's story reminds us that speed and simplicity are necessary for doing prototyping well. These are qualities that may be hard to maintain when an organization grows, becomes dominant, and acquires bureaucratic practices. The main insight that Magnus offers concerns the continuing importance of finding ways to connect to the client.

"Now we are a big, fat cat ourselves and really need to take special care to stay ahead. I'd love a place on our web were we could put out and test new functionalities without fully integrating them. We need to still be fast in responding, first with smart uses of new technology, and above all, remain close to the client. That's just extremely important. It's so easy to get lost. You've got to be close to be first."

"Now I have been away from the market for some time. I want to ask a trader if I can sit with him or her for a full day again, just to feel what they are concerned with now, what they care about and ask for. You are there for the trader. So if you manage to meet his needs for an entire day, you are doing well. Close to the client, close to the client, close to the client, I'd say those are the three things at the top."

A FEW HOURS

One may think that rapid prototyping is a work practice that is particular to design firms or others engaging in formal product development, like Point Carbon. It is not. Lawyers prototype their strategies for handling cases in the court. Journalists prototype their articles. Indeed, the journalists in *A-magasinet*, the leading weekend magazine that is distributed as a supplement to *Aftenposten*, are expected to work through a formalized prototype template before too much time and effort is invested in their articles. The more productive practice goes far beyond this – it is characterized by interaction around a high number of drafts. At first it might just be a title and a three-line summary shown to the two people sitting next to the journalist. Then comes a series of more elaborate drafts presented to a spouse, friends, and then to other colleagues. So by the time the article reaches print, the ideas in it may have come into contact with around thirty persons, and the main storyline may have been adjusted many times. The article, then, is the result of successive rounds of experiential learning through prototyping.

What about hydrocarbon exploration – surely that is a form of thorough science-based work that requires months, years, even decades? Yes, true enough, but prototyping still plays a major role. Without concretizing and testing new prospects (ideas for where oil and gas can be found), explorers may risk spending years going down unproductive alleys. Sometimes, a mere sketch on a piece of paper is all that it takes to involve others in your main idea.

A senior geologist in Houston nailed it after a workshop where six groups of explorers competed in prototyping prospects for the same area: "I used to think that we need unlimited amounts of time to find oil. Now I see that sometimes we can make do with a few hours". An exploration manager in Norway concurs: "Teams that don't function well are teams that keep on saying 'Oh, no, I need more data before I can take a stance on that.' Sometimes I need our best judgment within a week, no matter what."

Prototyping can involve not only clients and peers but also suppliers. During the Idea Work project, SpareBank 1 staged a number of workshops where its partners in information technology collaborated with in-house experts on specifying new payment systems. Small user scenarios representing voices of new client demands were also brought into the event. The prototype, then, has the function of assimilating many voices and testing their combined relevance in a speedy manner.

TESTING IN SINGLE AND DOUBLE LOOPS

Prototyping may ultimately concern imagining and testing user experiences. And rigorous testing is key. Without colleagues, friends or users looking critically at what is suggested, the cycle is not closed; their experiences are not sufficiently activated into what is produced. A prototype that is not tested through simulated or imagined use is dead in the water. But sometimes, testing is not enough unless one has doubled back to ask what particular needs or user experiences are targeted in the first place. Craig Dykers, head of Snøhetta's New York offices, puts this eloquently:

"Lately I have been intrigued by the fact that architecture is something that engenders memory. And memory is such a valuable thing in being human. I've had hundreds of meals in my lifetime, thousands and thousands of meals. I remember a few of them. And the reason why I remember them is based on a whole series of issues. Sometimes it's the company. Sometimes it's something unrelated to the food. Sometimes it's the food. And all of those things are what makes the event itself linger in my mind. I think that architecture is trying to do the same thing. I like to think that, as you say, the creation of a place where an experience can occur will engender memory, and therefore lodge itself firmly in the physicality of a human being. [...] First of all you need to think about which user experiences people should be able to have when they visit a building or a site. That comes prior to thinking form."

The key phrase here is "That comes prior to thinking form". Early prototypes may actually stifle idea work because one is not clear about which particular user experiences or, more generally, which problem spaces one is targeting. Starting with a building when the user needs are complex and uncertain, as is the case in the 9/11 Memorial Museum, may close down creativity rather than stimulate it. The dangerous shortcut here is trying to prototype exclusively in terms of some physical object rather than user experience or a larger issue. Prototyping can, for example, involve using images or metaphors or video images to imagine future   user experiences (Kelley 2005), *then* filling such imaginings with concrete products and services.

When rapid prototyping faces potential lock-in effects, we can say it needs to be "double" in the sense of first targeting a larger idea space before concrete solutions can be arrived at: What kind of user experience are we trying to meet? What kind of legal issue is this really? What kind of geological problem is this? Inspired by a year at film school, Magnus Køber once engaged in such double rapid prototyping by first imagining a day in a trader's life (to the point of creating a pamphlet), starting at 0700 in the morning, then specifying potential products and services for the trader throughout the day.

When does one know for certain when prototyping needs to be single or double? Probably seldom – and there are more single loops than double ones. But another thoughtful clue from Craig Dykers may be useful to keep in the back of our minds. To Craig, the user experiences one aims for should not be restricted to what the architects originally had in mind – one must get users, at least indirectly, to participate in the ideas:

"The best authors of architecture are creating a story that has different associations for the reader. [...] We did not talk about the glacier idea directly for the Norwegian Opera. You know, we're looking at this swan one day, and the shape of the swan, how beautiful it is. And how, when it sits on the water it just seems so majestic. And that shape of the Opera – if you look at it from elevation, it goes down and it comes back and it goes back. Nobody can see that. You'd have to tell them, and I'm glad that they don't see it, and that they are seeing it in another way. The more dualities you can build into a building, the more you increase the emotional space of the experience. I think you could apply that reasoning to anything. [...] If you're allowing for a broad range of experiences to coexist and work well together, that's basically the final answer to the question, I guess, when we have done our best work."

PROTOTYPING DYLAN:
THE WITMARK SESSIONS

Very early in his career, from 1962 to 1964, as songs tumbled out of him at an incredible rate, Bob Dylan would go into the Look Building on 51st Street, Manhattan's Tin Pan Alley in New York, and make demos of his songs for the aptly-named music executive, Artie Mogull. You can hear these demos in their unmixed form on *The Witmark Demos: Bootleg Series Vol. 9*, titled for the publishing company, M. Witmark & Sons, where Dylan recorded them. These are fragments of songs, designs for songs, songs in the making. Some of the songs are interrupted and incomplete: Dylan forgets the words at times or stops in mid-verse, thinking of a better line that he could use. The demo sessions took place in a tiny six-by-eight-foot studio at Witmark's offices and were recorded on a reel-to-reel tape deck. The demos were recorded at 7.5 inches per second, half the speed used in professional studios; consequently there is a lot of background noise and occasional tape hiss. The lyrics and music were transcribed from the tape to create song sheets mailed out to recording companies. When an artist expressed an interest in a song, an acetate recording on inexpensive plastic would be sent to the artist for preview purposes. If acceptable, the song would be recorded. The point of the sessions was Dylan laying his tunes and words down so they could be translated into sheet music, which other artists, such as Odetta or Peter, Paul and Mary, would then record.

These Witmark sessions were never meant for public consumption. "Do you want this? It's awful long," he asks near the end of "Let Me Die in My Footsteps." "It's not that it's long, it's that it's a drag. I sang it so many times." But despite the poor quality production values and variable performances, *The Witmark Demos* are fascinating documents, capturing Dylan's first burst of creativity. Prototypes appear of songs that would never see the light of day, along with styles that he tried out and then rejected.

Although the Witmark sessions are a testament to rapid prototyping, the prototypes were not dropped after initial specification. Nor were they de novo creations when they were first prototyped – they drew heavily on prior traditions and works. Not all these songs were "new"; in fact many of them were old. They had already been prototyped many times before Dylan laid his hands on them. A case in point is "Baby Let Me follow You Down", which provided Dylan with his first rock cover by the Animals, an R&B group from Newcastle, UK. The song was first recorded in 1930 and had a call-and-response form, featuring Memphis Minnie and Joe McCoy. Dylan credits the song to three more contemporary composers, Eric Von Schmidt, the Reverend Gary Davis, and Dave Van Ronk, although he explicitly names Von Schmidt from whom he says he first learned it in the "green pastures" of Harvard University. Between Memphis Minnie and Von Schmidt there were many other versions. Michael Gray (2006: p.28) lists some of the best known. After recording it during the Witmark sessions, Dylan didn't let the song go; it pops up in the Manchester Free Trade Hall concert on 17 May 1966 in an electrifying rock version. The number is typical of Dylan's prototyping and of prototyping in general. There is an early tryout, developed itself from ideas already in good currency. Over successive iterations, the idea is reworked and re-honed in performance. The prototype is never finished, set in concrete. It continues to evolve and has been occasionally revisited over the years.

As in Dylan's case, successful prototyping always has an element of the improvised performance.

TIPS FOR PRACTICE

1. *Ask fundamental questions of problem space* to avoid lock in and invite a double loop: What kinds of possibilities, problems, and/or user experiences do our prototyping address?

2. *Use different kinds of boundary objects* to exchange ideas, particularly sketches; but also images, physical models, and stories of user experiences. Variation increases the space of possibility. Boundary objects have different functions in testing particular aspects of the ideas that are half-finished, thereby enlarging the space for extended sharing and co-creation.

3. *Stage parallel prototyping* by producing alternative prototypes for sharing, genuine and fast feedback, and further development – for example, by letting groups compete in half-day to full-day sessions. Avoid take-it-or-leave-it. Maintain competing models even when projects mature, sometimes even after market launch.

4. *Pitch presentations early* in the course of things before it's too late. Show the rough sketches, the cheap foam model, and half-written notes.

5. *Have available tools and material* at your workstation, in social zones, and in meeting rooms. You can go a long way with Post-Its and a Sharpie.

6. *Involve internal and/or external users* at an early stage, for example through:

    • Arranging for informal exchanges with lead users and decision makers

    • Organizing multi-client development projects on new applications

    • Prototyping analysis; Fast first versions, client discussions, updates

    • Standing in user shoes: Imagining the day of a user and placing one's ideas in that story, looking over the shoulder of users, simulating being a user, maybe shaking them up a little

    • Creating low-threshold channels for eliciting user feedback: Webinars, user group meetings, chat platforms, hotlines

THINGS TO AVOID

Always asking for more time, more resources, more data, more everything. Following the linear path: analyze, develop, produce and ship it, *then* asking for feedback. Bureaucracy. Lack of autonomy. Paralysis by analysis. Seeking early and inward-looking perfection. Forgetting to test things; mere talk is cheap, and lists of ideas on the wall are completely useless unless something is done with them. Fail rarely and you'll learn slowly!

READINGS FOR
LEARNING AND INSPIRATION

Many of the best practical sources on rapid prototyping come from the Silicon Valley, fed in particular by the collaboration between Stanford's Design School and IDEO, a world-leading design firm. While there is also literature on prototyping in manufacturing and software design, the Stanford/IDEO tradition is very useful because it offers conceptions and practices that seem relevant to any kind of idea work.

Brown, T. (2009). *Change by Design: How Design Thinking Transforms Organizations and Inspires Innovation*. New York, NY: Harper Collins. [A contemporary but classic statement of the need to bring design thinking and business intelligence into constructive dialogue and simultaneous development with each other, written by the current CEO of IDEO.]

Clegg, S. R., Carter, C, Kornberger, M. and Schweitzer, J. (2011). *Strategy: Theory & Practice*. London: Sage. [An introduction to "strategy" that incorporates some of the latest ideas about design thinking and prototyping.]

Dylan, B. (2010) *The Bootleg Series Vol. 9 – The Witmark Demos: 1962-1964*. New York, NY: Columbia. [Prototypes of music history.]

Ford, C. (2009). Prototyping processes that affect organizational creativity, in R. Tudor, M. A. Runco and S. Moger (eds.), *The Routledge Companion to Creativity*. London: Routledge. [A conceptual paper on prototyping that places the practice in an evolutionary theory of creativity.]

Gray, M. (2006). *The Bob Dylan Encyclopedia*. New York, NY: Continuum. [A compendium for fans, by a fan, one who is also an erudite scholar.]

Kelly, T. and Littman, J. (2000). *The Art of Innovation: Lessons in Creativity from IDEO, America's Leading Design Firm*. New York, NY: Doubleday [An early book on the practices of IDEO from one of its founders, a book that preceded the Design Thinking tradition, see chapter 6 on prototyping.]

Kelley, T. (2005). *The Ten Faces of Innovation*. New York Broadway Business. [Another highly practical book by Kelley describing in detail a range of practices that are complementary to prototyping.]

Kolb, D. (1984). *Experiential Learning: Experience as the Source of Learning and Development*. Englewood Cliffs, NJ: Prentice Hall. [The classic text on experiential learning, there are a number of useful recent summaries, see for example: http://www.infed.org/biblio/b-explrn.htm.]

Lamott, A. (1995). *Bird by Bird: Some Instructions on Writing and Life*. New York, NY: Anchor Books [Not a book on prototyping per se but rather on the craft of writing. In the full spirit of prototyping, Lamott introduces the practices of "writing really, really, really shitty drafts" and breaking down her work into very managable small steps.]

Leonardi, P. (2011). Early prototypes can hurt a team's productivity. *Harvard Business Review,* December, 28. [A usefull reminder of why prototyping sometimes needs to double back.]

Sims. P. (2011). *Little Bets: How Breakthrough Ideas Emerge from Small Discoveries*. New York, NY: Free Press. [This book is remarkable for being about prototyping while managing to take a step back and place it in a larger tradition of experiential learning and experimental innovation.]

EXERCISES

1. What ideas are you working on right now? How could you make them tangible so that others might grasp them?

2. What different forms do you think prototypes can take?

3. When do you think prototyping should be double loop versus single loop?

4. How do you see the role of stories in prototyping?

5. How could you involve your clients/end-users more in your prototyping efforts?

6. Rapid prototyping means giving a voice to other experts, to customers, and to colleagues; What risks do you think this might pose and how would you overcome them?

7. Looking to the other qualities of extraordinary idea work, how do you think rapid prototyping relates to generative resistance or to liberating laughter? Is prototyping confined to particulars, or could it be a part of the process of zooming out?

8. Looking to theories of experiential learning, how is prototyping an example of something larger - that is, what other ways do you think there are to learn rapidly and become smarter from one's experience?

9. Think of the work that you do. Now explain it in terms that an eight-year-old child might understand. If you can do that, you can prototype.

LIBERATING LAUGHTER

HOW PLAYFULL ENERGY AND HUMOR OPENS UP PEOPLE, SITUATIONS, AND IDEAS

ARNE CARLSEN, AINA LANDSVERK HAGEN[1]
STEWART CLEGG AND REIDAR GJERSVIK

lib·er·at·ing laugh·ter |
Processes of energizing co-creation through playfulness, puns, and humor that build social ties, ease seriousness, relax constraints in thinking, and encourage original combinations of knowledge.

Jenny is a person with strong likes and dislikes. Landscapes + architecture: this is what excites her, as her dreams roam outside and between the spaces that her interdisciplinary architect colleagues create at Snøhetta. Jenny, as a landscape architect, differentiates between what exists, the contexts (plants, rocks, surface), and what is changed or new (buildings, roads, bridges). The ability to combine these worldviews, she explains, is what is exciting about being an architect at Snøhetta.

The retracing of Jenny's professional life is done in the middle of a busy dockside warehouse, a large open space now colonized by architects, where we sit on the quite uncomfortable orange sofa positioned as a nucleus in the office of Snøhetta. "A bad idea? It doesn't exist." That's Jenny's verdict on ideas. Asked to define an idea, she laughs, like an erupting volcano, blazing through the soundscape of the huge warehouse building, her hah, hah, hah raising the general decibel level on a normal working day to maximum volume.

> "What's an idea? Ah, oh my God. You are definitely doing research! This might take some time! Ha, ha, ha!!"

She is clearly amused by the direct, disturbingly difficult question. *What Is an Idea?* There is a split second of silence, followed by "oi, oi, oi". And then, leaning forward, Jenny explains: "It is a type of answer." [pause] "... Even better, a possibility." She articulates the words slowly, but precisely. "It's rarely an end product, though. More often it's the first spark, the light bulb, a first indication of something that can evolve over time with input from several people." Throughout her career, ideas have been experienced like this.

Jenny talks about one of these sparks being lit when working in Gambia on the university campus in Faraba Banta where the team of architects fought and quarreled over what became the essential idea – a fractal building structure inspired by the West African way of constructing space. "These elements, repeated in greater elements, like what you see in the pattern on their clothes or instruments... we were all hooked on that idea", Jenny energetically exclaims. "Well, all of us except one of the team members, who didn't really like the basic idea". Speaking of this opposition she says, "it forced us to refine and strengthen the concept that argued for it. The *energy* used to accentuate the idea was formidable".

When interviewing Jenny this word, *energy*, pops up again and again, both through her vocal sparks and as a recurring impression. *Energy.* It is gathered, lost, gained and used, it comes in all sizes and shapes in conversations in which Jenny participates. Energy comes from digressions, from direct discussions with clients, from the one-to-one testing of models with engineers or the dynamics between team members. At the core of such energizing interactions, at the core of Jenny's ways, there is laughter. Jenny's sense of humor and fun in her work is infectious; indeed, it is one of the most noticeable things about her.

SERIOUS PLAY AND LIBERATING LAUGHTER

Jenny personifies idea work as serious play. It is play not as separate activities of Lego-building or going rafting together, but attitudes and behavior characterized by playfulness and laughter that are embedded in everyday value-producing activities. The notion of idea work as serious play is particularly true in at least three ways.

First, idea work inevitably has to operate under ambiguous circumstance and tough constraints, sometimes, contradictory ones, and the very activity of producing something new means opposing something old. Thus idea work in all its hardship and seriousness must be experienced as *liberating* and *energizing*. As witnessed in ongoing projects, the introduction of particularly challenging constraints in projects, the need for building a screen around a new office building – immediately elicits playful responses, like nominating screen kings and screen queens. The more serious the business, the more the need for play.

And as told by the partner, director and board member of Snøhetta, Ole Gustavsen:

> "We encounter so many challenging problems in our profession, and I'd much rather interact with someone who handles hardship with a relaxed and playful attitude. You always want to reconnect with those persons."

Jenny's laughter is so valuable in idea work because it is invitational, associative, liberates from hardship, and energizes people.

We do not know if Jenny has read the literary philosopher Mikhail Bakhtin, famous for his theory of carnivalesque laughter as a liberating, renewing force. To Bakhtin, laughter, ridicule, festivities, swearing, and the use of the grotesque in carnivals functioned as a challenge to the meaning of authority and power. Through liberating laughter, people are able take the high and mighty down from their pinnacle and into the gutter to create meaning anew. But Jenny probably does not need to read Bakhtin because she already knows the essential truth he tries to tell us:

"True ambivalent and universal laughter does not deny seriousness, but purifies and completes it. Laughter purifies from dogmatism, from the intolerant and the petrified; it liberates from fanaticism and pedantry, from fear and intimidation, from didacticism, naïveté and illusion, from single meaning, the single level, from sentimentality. Laughter does not permit seriousness to atrophy and to be torn away from the one being, forever incomplete. It restores this ambivalent wholeness."

Mikhail Bakhtin (1984: pp. 122–123), *Rabelais and His World*

HUMBLE FEARLESS
DOERS HAVING FUN

Second, idea work is serious play because evoking laughter is the cousin of all creation. The basic mechanisms is the same: *bi-sociation* (Koestler 1964/1989). In its simplest sense, this means combining things that few people would think belong together. More principally, bi-sociation means perceiving a situation, an event, or a set of data from two incompatible frames of references or models.

The rise of Point Carbon as a pioneer in the carbon market trade and a major player in the power and gas market can be seen as precisely stemming from the ability to combine three sets of competences that no-one had combined before: knowledge of trading, knowledge of climate change policies, and knowledge of advanced mathematical modeling. Point Carbon's operative motto and identity statement is "humble fearless doers having fun". It bespeaks the playfulness necessary to foster new combinations. More specifically, the analysts at Point Carbon brought their sense of play to creating new terms that defined the carbon market:

"People who used to work with climate change policies were now in a trading environment. Everything was new and there was only a vague understanding about what the carbon market would look like. We had to come up with concepts and terms that worked. It's a very playful form of thinking, like the terms 'crack spread' or 'emission to cap'. It's cool, a touch of double meaning, it's fun. It was a very heavy academic approach to things, while simultaneously being tabloid and very clear about playing in the market. So you cannot play too much. It must not be perceived as flippancy, being disrespectful. You must be able to show a very clear argument behind it all. A lot of the things in our analysis are still fun. The process of coming up with titles on a report, simple things like naming figures, trying to be fun and cunning, somewhat word games-like."

FINDING THE TONE

A third way in which idea work is serious play has to do with team interactions. Asked about what distinguishes a brilliant versus a mediocre exploration team, Dan Tuppen, an exploration manager in the northern-most office of Statoil, in Harstad, reflected on a puzzling experience. Two project teams in exploration, seemingly identical in terms of composition (mix of disciplines and experiences), tasks (deliverables and timelines), and enabling resources (data, work space, technology), performed very differently. In the low-performing team, people started to prioritize other projects, were reluctant to participate in meetings, and hardly ever showed up in the designated locale. Engagement more or less fizzled out. By contrast, people in the high-performing team could not wait to engage in meetings, spent most of their working day together, and delivered beyond expectations. Struggling with understanding the dynamics that created this difference, Dan lands on *tone*:

> "Each team has to find its tone in a way. I believe humour is very important, in particular if we are in a stressful situation. Then we need to create a little distance. It is wrong to say it is like 'not giving a shit'. Rather it's like making small humorous provocations in the situation, what I would call in English 'banter'. Practical jokes may be part of it, and also self-irony. The clue is to get the banter tone in the team. Then work is faster, more efficient, we handle pressure and people are fully engaged."

It is key to Dan's reasoning here that it is not the singular joke or isolated pun that sets the right tone. Rather, it is the *atmosphere* of laughter that makes the difference, a history of a series of small and large acts and the anticipation of more. Such an atmosphere of laughter may well be the signature practice of a very good team, or team meeting. We were at first surprised when Senior Vice President in Statoil Exploration, Pål Haremo repeatedly insisted that, "every truly good meeting has at least one outburst of roaring laughter!" – or when Ole Gustavsen of Snøhetta claimed that liberating laughter is the most fundamental of all the qualities of extraordinary idea work. These views make perfect sense if we talk of liberating laughter in the plural and acknowledge the many kinds of laughter required for idea work to sparkle. We may say then that an atmosphere welcoming of laughter can involve the playful laughter of prototyping, the light laughter involved in shedding weight and zooming out, the enchanted or worried laughter that follows wonder, the disarming laughter that rounds out tough critique and eases the seriousness of drama, or the audacious laughter of punk production. It is precisely in this way that we may return to the words of Bakhtin and see that liberating laughter does not deny seriousness, but restores and completes it.

JESTERS AND NAKEDNESS

The institutionalizing of laughter in the form of court jesters may be seen as a very old organizational practice, one that has modern manifestations in the likes of Dilbert or John Stewart. The fool presents mirrors in which people see their mistakes without having to admit to them. Because of that, our foolish laughter has the power not only to generate new ideas but also to escape from the old, an escape that entails stripping the patina of received wisdom from ideas waiting to be revealed. Välikangas and Sevón (2010) describe the process most playfully in a recent paper:

> "Only fools (and perhaps children, as in Hans Andersen's story of the emperor's missing clothes) can be forgiven the unique privilege, without demolishing the social order, of pointing out the (too) obvious, the forbidden, and the partially hidden, and making the ideas that embody us and that we perform, albeit sometimes unknowingly, visible. A jester facilitates the undressing of such masquerades. A good jester's wit then, also serves as a lubricant to the reckoning. The nakedness that would be rejected off-hand, were it not coated with humor, now becomes more palatable." (Välikangas and Sevón, 2010: p. 150)

Good jesters don't suffer fools. Think of Shakespeare's King Lear, and the role the Jester plays. Lear's Jester is a symbol of decency, common sense, and honesty – one of the few able to speak truth to power. He has an implicit license to kill foolishness and takes advantage of this license to mock, speak freely, dispense frank observations, highlighting the folly of Lear and his flawed judgments. For the Jester there is the privilege of undercutting, ironizing, and mocking the powers that be and their authoritative views. In the company of sycophants sabotage sometimes succeeds when fools rush in where the wise may fear to tread.

TIPS FOR PRACTICE

1. *Encourage banter*, puns, riddles, and practical jokes in everyday team work to facilitate team spirit and release from seriousness.

2. *Cherish your Jennys* and celebrate energizing behavior through informal awards or other forms of recognition. To cherish people such as Jenny organizations have to show that they are seriously polyphonic – that they welcome internal opposition, that crazy ideas, no matter how far off the wall, are worth consideration.

3. *Play with the established jargon* of your organization (or industry/sector) and its traditions, and *bi-sociate*: seek reversal of logic and inversions of concepts and assumptions by identifying and exploring seemingly incompatible models or frames of reference. For example, play with words; explore metaphors, try free associations, try new and wild combinations of things that break with normalcy and have no other apparent quality than that they seem cool and interesting.

4. *Create and mark space for play,* for example by ritualizing creative sessions and using objects as social markers for untamed exploration, e.g., a piece of chocolate for informal sparring or a green flag or hat for free associations.

5. *Use play rituals to level the field* when someone dominates or otherwise exerts power that limits people: for example, give everyone a fixed number of straws, with each one entitling the holder to speak. Once the straws are used up, there are no more legitimate rights to speak – this can do wonders for positive power relations in a group!

6. *Institutionalize the role of the jester* by performing show numbers or slapstick acts, or even better: as part of projects. In Snøhetta, every project group has a "groupie" that is invited to observe and listen to the team's ideas and reflections at regular intervals during the project period. This person is not part of the team per se, as he or she is supposed to provide the outsiders view on the process. The groupie is expected to criticize, enrich, and bolster ideas as well as provide solutions for the creative process of the team.

7. *Conduct ritual cleansing* of non-discussable issues and bad habits by exposing them and parodying them. Examples include introducing anti-narratives exaggerate complaining habits or staging ritual burials of old ideas/methods/habits.

THINGS TO AVOID

Seriousness without laughter, for example allowing someone to be
too assertive because they claim status based on position or authority.
Laughter without seriousness: the irony trap of ridiculing everything and
never making any commitments, or believing that laughter without deep
knowledge leads to innovation. Laughing *at* people instead of *with* them:
cynical, scornful laughter is not liberating at all – it ruins relationships
and brings death to creative efforts.

RESOURCES FOR
LEARNING AND INSPIRATION

Bakhtin, M. (1984). *Rabelais and His world*. Bloomington: Indiana University Press. [This is the dissertation work of the Russian linguist and philosopher Mikhail Bakhtin. It is one of the most cited and famous books of all of social science and portrays a history of laughter as seen by the social institution of the carnival and the grotesque in medieval Europe. Carnival stands for a range of symbolic realms that includes dancing, feasting, include wearing of bizarre dress, use of alcohol and engagement of the material lower body stratum. To Bakhtin, cultivating carnivalesque laughter was a road to knowledge, ultimately about the victory of the future over the past, in becoming, change and renewal.]

Cooper, C., and Sosik, J. (2011). The laughter advantage: Cultivating high quality connections and workplace outcomes through humor. In K. Cameron and G. Spreitzer (Eds.). *Handbook of Positive Organizational Scholarship*. (pp. 474–489). New York, NY: Oxford University Press. [A fine recent review on the role of humor in the work place, with particular emphasis of how humor is relational and can foster high quality connections.]

Dutton, J. E. (2003). *Energize Your Workplace: How to Create and Sustain High-Quality Connections at Work*. San Francisco, CA: Jossey-Bass. [A brilliant and highly accessible practitioner-oriented book on energizing more than laughter. This book preceded much later research on high quality connections. The section on respectful engagement is particularly profound, wide awake with vivid examples and insightful advice.]

Gray, D., Brown, S., and Macanufo, J. (2010). *GameStorming, A Playbook for Innovators, Rulebreakers and Change-makers*. Sebastopol, CA: O'Reilly. [A playful and practital guide to use of games in idea work, including games for not just idea generation but also prioritization, closing, convergence, and experimentation. See also http://www.gogamestorm.com/]

Koestler, A. (1964/1989). *The Act of Creation*. Harmondsworth: Penguin. [The classic text of Koestler preceded much contemporary work on knowledge combination and brokering. Still relevant and quite accessible, the first 100 pages or so deals with the role of humour in the creative act.]

Mainemelis, B., and Ronson, S. (2006). Ideas are born in fields of play: Toward a theory of play and creativity in organizational settings. *Research in Organizational Behavior*, 27: 81–131. [This is an excellent recent review article on play in idea work, particularly strong on the role of play in building social ties.]

Välikangas, L., and Sevón, G. (2010). Of managers, ideas and jesters, and the role of information technology. *The Journal of Strategic Information Systems*, 19: 145–153. [A feisty and entertaining account about the need for playfulness in idea work, particularly interesting with regards to the age-old institution of jesters and their modern manifestations in today's organizations.]

Sandelands, L. E. (2010). The play of change. *Journal of Organizational Change Management* 23(1): 71–86. [A beautiful paper on the embodied nature of play, why play is central in all change, and why it is a form of love.]

Schrage, M. (2000). *Serious Play*. Cambridge, MA: Harvard Business School Press. [A practitioner-oriented book that is excellent in capturing playful practices and spirits of idea work at MIT.]

Shakespeare, W. (1608/2012). King Lear. http://ebooks.adelaide.edu.au/s/shakespeare/william/lear/, accessed 28th September, 2012. [One of Shakespeare's late tragedies and political plays, with implications for all organizations, especially those governed by family gerontocracies. Imagine the role of Lear played by Rupert Murdoch, for example. Seeing his performances before the House of Commons serves as a good rehearsal of the potential.]

EXERCISES

1. Define up to five key major barriers to extraordinary idea work and discuss how laughter can be liberating to each one of them.

2. What do you think is the relationship between energizing behavior and laughter? Are the two always connected?

3. Pick up a copy of the recent biography on Steve Jobs and read through the first two chapters. In their formative years, the two founders of Apple, Jobs and Wozniack, were both renowned for their repeated pranks. How do you think those pranks mattered to their idea work?

4. Looking back at your own most successful idea work – whether alone or in projects – can you think of examples of when laughter in some way enabled collective performance? Vice versa – can you think of examples when laughter stifled performance?

5. Looking ahead towards future idea work projects, describe as concretely as possible what you would try in order to achieve the right tone of liberating, productive laughter in the team.

6. Looking across to other qualities of idea work: Pick any three of the other qualities of extraordinary idea work and try to specify how liberating laughter could enable them.

7. Looking to theory on creativity, innovation, or organizational change: To what degree do you think the idea of liberating laughter is discussed in the dominant literature? What key contributions in that regard are not mentioned here?

GENERATIVE RESISTANCE

HOW CONSTRAINTS AND OPPOSITION CAN INSPIRE YOUR BEST IDEAS

ARNE CARLSEN, STEWART CLEGG AND REIDAR GJERSVIK

gen·er·a·tive re·sist·ance |
Aknowledging doubt, friction, anomalies, and critique, not
as noise to be avoided, but levers to question the given and
enhance imagination in everyday work.

> "The living state of doubt drives and energizes us to generate possibilities, try them out, modify, transform or abandon them, try again, and so on, until new concepts or patterns are generated that productively satisfy our doubt."

Locke, Golden-Biddle and Feldman (2008: p. 908). *Making doubt generative*

To most people who meet her, Marianne Sætre comes across as a wise lady. "Wow, that was a wise person; a fine human being; that was incredibly well put", people say. Many have had conversations with her, heard her give presentations or lectures at universities. Marianne is Senior Architect and a long-time employee of Snøhetta, and has been an integral member of Snøhetta's most prestigious projects. She comes across as a causally laid back woman who favors the prototypical look of creatives worldwide, with black clothing matching her jet-black ponytail, sometimes an elegant dress; at other times designer jeans. Marianne frequently says that creativity is a place where one arrives only after having done a lot of prepping, a room that you can enter only after lots of effort, and a place that some people never manage to access. You do not just walk, freely, into that room: in order to enter you have to be able to seek, confront, and resist:

> "This contradiction, or the resistance that arises – you've got to use it as a positive feature. You need resistance to establish an understanding of the energy that is inherent in the project you have born. Creativity is really about having the courage to ask the right questions: where is the resistance in the project?"

BARCODE B10.1

In 2007, Snøhetta was commissioned to design an office building, "Barcode B10.1", on the site that lies on the west side of the Station Commons in Oslo: The Barcode Project. From the start the project faced many regulatory restrictions, such as sightlines, building codes, and spatial relations to public space, making the design task a constant struggle.
The Barcode complex was to be located along what was being developed as Oslo's new seafront, a phoenix rising out of the ashes of heavy industry that once occupied the site. Development of outdoor refreshment facilities with a view of the fjord was part of the contract.

"In Barcode B10.1 a whole range of external conditions presented unshakable boundaries to what we could do, everything from a sight corridor enforced by the Directorate of Cultural Heritage to the distance to adjacent buildings, different terrain levels, elements that were needed in the building, an already designed city space at the Station Common, and the work space needs of the users. There was an incredible amount of conditions that needed to be dealt with. We started like we always do, discussing what the possibilities were, how we could achieve the quality that inspires us and creates faith, and at the same time, how we could meet the challenge of the many limitations and boundary conditions. The interesting thing that happened was that something started to take form in the intersection between what we wanted and what we were able to do and what was possible and what the limits were. The solution grew out of the encounter with everything that was impossible."

The design of Barcode B10.1 developed from the tension between the internal room design, the external limitations, and a desire to create a building that would be sculptural in form. The proposed building design sought to comply with the Barcode principles and regulations, but it introduced in addition an interaction of surfaces on the horizontal and vertical planes. The sight corridor stipulated in the planning regulations limited the height of the buildings in a field that cuts across the roof toward Ekebergåsen, the northwestern part of the Ekeberg hill, located behind the city, as seen from the fjord. A cross connection was to be maintained from the Stations Common. A vertical split rotates through the building and connects the cross section to a sculptural, internal structure materialized as a cleft in the façade, with a view to the fjord. Marianne notes:

> "We ended up making this really interesting inside sculptural form.
> It was generated, for example, by how the sight corridor crosses the
> building diagonally, and the thought that the work spaces needed
> internal relations. It became an internal atrium of sorts; a twisted
> shape that is expressed in the facade and provides contact internally,
> an outside-in and inside-out quality that gives something back to the city.
> The key was to separate this sculptural form from the support system."

Buildings with cleft facades are not an easy design choice. They present substantial design and construction issues that have to be dealt with. As Marianne says, "Our work processes cannot be understood as linear. We keep coming back to things, constantly testing and revising the choices made". These choices always face constraints.

The idea of generative resistance counters a widespread implicit "harmony model" of creative efforts: namely, that available knowledge, sufficient resources, and mutual support and trust are what it takes to be creative. In Marianne's world, people do not become creative by agreeing with each other; it is their considered and intelligently reasoned disagreement, debate, and difference that drive innovation. Making resistance generative is not about what is easy or pleasant, but entails actively seeking out, exploring, and using what is difficult.

Generative resistance relies on the use of a network of mutual resistance – people who can resist and be resisted. Marianne represents a type of idea worker who thrives on difference, on polyphony. A good workplace for her is one in which she is working with people with whom she can disagree creatively. This two-way struggle – a dialectic – of creative power and creative resistance means that it is important for the organization to inculcate a tolerance of differences, an assertion of ideas against resistance. Borrowing from the French philosopher, Jean-Luc Nancy, the dialectic requires "resistance to the communion of everyone or to the exclusive passion of one or several of kindred spirits" (Nancy 1991: p. 35) rather than a simple clash of adversaries. It is only in this way that the positive power of polyphony can be unleashed and resistance that is truly generative can unfold.

Idea work can be life-enhancing and deeply rewarding, but that does not mean that it is all about organizational peace, love, and understanding. On the contrary, idea work seldom plays out as a harmonious, step-by-step sequence of events, where ingenious ideas readily spring forth out of mutually supportive and joyful interactions. Instead, the ideas that matter are often hard-wrung, fraught with anxiety, and emergent after periods of standstill and hardship. Generative resistance signifies practices that entail confrontation with others' strategies and determinations. It means entering the sometimes ruthless arenas of competitive ideas – such as architectural competitions, tough legal battles, and getting prospects for finding oil to be nominated as drill candidate against a half a dozen internal competitors. The point is to use confrontations, roadblocks, doubts and questions not as negative constraints, but as valuable levers for bringing energy into interaction and movement into thinking.

Idea work without generative resistance is lifeless. It is tempting to avoid asking questions that may confront previous understanding. It is tempting to believe that what someone else did on some matter is much better than what we can do ourselves. And it is tempting to escape from bewilderment and ambiguities by jumping to conclusions prematurely. Many might welcome such shortcuts but to do so would not be wise, according to Marianne. For her, it is a privilege to have her ideas challenged. "Most things really worth creating do not come to us easily. If they had, others would probably have created them already", says Marianne:

> "Barcode B10.1 became great because it arose in the intersection of resistance between all the boundary conditions. That is where its creative force came from. We never would have designed it like that, never would have found that form, without that resistance."

RESISTING THE INEVITABILITY OF DEFEAT, THE DOMINANCE OF MODELS, AND THE VIEWS OF CLIENTS

The two representatives from competing banks had just stepped outside for a smoke during the tender process for a major cash management contract for the city of Trondheim. "I remember him saying something I thought quite derogatory at the time", said Thor Ragnar Klevstuen of Sparebank 1:

> "He suggested we should leave the overall tender to the big banks – how could we possibly win anyhow? – and concentrate instead on handling only the payment for social clients. When back at our offices, I told Per Oskar Olsen, the manager of our cash management portfolio, about the event. Per Oskar thought about it for a few seconds, then looked at me insistently and said: 'Well, do you know what, Thor? That's just precisely how we are going to win the whole contract. Handling the payments for social clients is the difficult thing; the rest is standard business.' So we went ahead and concentrated our efforts there and won that contract. And now, well, as you know, this has matured into huge development efforts for handling similar cases with cash cards and other things. And it all started from that comment!"

The experiences of Snøhetta and SpareBank 1 mirror that of hydrocarbon exploration. The history of discoveries at Statoil and other oil companies offers abundant examples of breakthrough ideas emerging from forceful questioning of established truths and dominant exploration models. Most major discoveries seem to come in areas that have been explored for many years based on what later proved to be wrong models. The key to new discoveries is often "understanding why the previous wells did not work". Successful exploration, then, is often based on the ability to come up with an alternative geological model based on the data from dry wells. A culture of questioning is key to success. As stated by an explorer who had just made a major discovery in an area presumed bereft of oil:

> "In our group there is a lot of leeway – this doesn't mean that you sit inside your office and ponder on your own and then come out once in a while. There is a constant input of ideas and questions from others. Then oops, you see things entirely differently. It's an atmosphere of constant turmoil with lots of regional maps and coffee and loud voices. My colleagues really ask the best questions... you need that wondering type of person [who is asking]: '*why* is it like that, *why* is it so?' [... to] have an explorative mind, wanting to know how things work [...] not just stating that this is how it is, but asking '*why, why?*'"

One can see the same patterns in the client interactions at Thommessen on complicated legal issues. As one key corporate client said, when praising lawyers for being critical and inquisitive, offering counterviews: "We want resistance and to be challenged. It makes us better. It makes us feel safe that we have made the right choices. If one only gives in, insecurity results."

SOCIAL SPACE,
KNOWLEDGE AND COURAGE

Having the guts to seek out the toughest challenges and then meeting them is one thing. Another is to create sufficient room for criticism. Not all teams function in the same way as the petroleum explorers mentioned above do, nor do all teams have clients similar to Thommessen. Challenges often have a human face, a representative who speaks for their inflexibility. So the resistance can become personal for both givers and takers. Egos are easily bruised. It takes courage to speak out against star performers. It takes personal strength to bounce back from creative deconstructions, and it takes an inner calm to be able to process all the useful points of resistance that the others raise. The trick seems to be to install practices where people are allowed to resist wisely, creatively, so that friction becomes a stimulus for imagination. Creating a social space for criticism entails at least temporary tolerance of direct disagreement and tough scrutiny, and that the critique of ideas is done in respectful and energizing ways.

In hydrocarbon exploration, all prospects that end up being drilled go through several rounds of formalized peer reviews, with designated roles for reviewers who master a variety of sub-disciplines and/or possess broad regional knowledge. Statoil's chief geologist may have been involved in all drilling ideas at some stage, assuming a role of providing criticism and assistance based on the experience of having succeeded themselves and having seen hundreds of previous ideas being tested. The role is similar to that of a chief editor overseeing a portfolio of reviews in top academic journals. In Snøhetta, every project group has someone known colloquially as a "groupie" that is invited to observe and listen to the team's ideas and reflections at regular intervals during the project period. This person is not a member of the team per se, because he or she is expected to provide an outsider's view, criticize and strengthen ideas. A related and less time-consuming practice is to set off limited periods of time in meetings or workshops during which direct criticism is strongly encouraged.

None of these practices work without the deep knowledge and personal investment of the people providing resistance. While well-known approaches such as de Bono's provocative operations (de Bono 1992) may be useful, generative resistance cannot be reduced to a set of generic techniques that work independently of their users. It is simply not that easy. Imagine that you are sitting in an idea work session, and a star performer enters the room. Her presence unintentionally quells debate. The star offers an idea that is quite promising but really, you feel, it is just not good enough. In such a situation, how would you mobilize resistance that could be generative?

FLOWS OF TRADITION AND FLOWS OF RESISTANCE IN IDEAS ABOUT OURSELVES

Resistance to received ideas requires imagining the grounds of how they came to be and the possibility of them being different. Sometimes fates flow in ways that open our eyes.

Many of the great cities in the world are defined by watercourses that etch their shifting contours into the landscape. The Thames is one such river. In 2012 it became the central icon in two contrasting spectacles. On a cold, wet, and dreary day, it hosted a flotilla of boats watched from some distance by spectators. One of these vessels carried the members of the British royal family, and the Monarch herself waved to the watching crowds. This was tradition writ large: subjects watched their Queen gliding by on the Thames, and cheered her reign, implicitly accepting their role as subjects in a ceremony that, apart from the modernish appearance of some of the vessels, could just as well have been a ceremonial procession in feudal times – loyal subjects paying tribute by watching and applauding their distant and unspeaking Monarch, fleetingly glimpsed, under dreary skies.

A few weeks later, the Thames was again featured as an icon in the pageant that opened the London Olympics. The river route was followed from where it springs from the ground to the East End of London, where the games' site was located, with David Beckham, an ex-footballer, carrying the Olympic Torch on the last stage, handing it over at the stadium to a group of seven young athletes, identities unknown, ordinary people, citizens of tomorrow, not yet famous. The sentiment deflating the usual speculations about which great British subject would carry the flame to its final destination was perfectly in harmony with a pageant that could hardly have been more generatively resistant to the political traditions of both the opening ceremonies and the representations of British life under a Conservative government. The only character missing was Karl Marx, working on his critique of political economy, *Capital*, in the British Museum. What he criticized was evident: the dark Satanic mills, the bosses in top hats counting their money, and the workers in cloth caps, in their masses. Marx's legacy was present also: the Jarrow Marchers, who were led by a founding member of the British Communist Party, Ellen Wilkinson; the National Health Service, represented by hundreds of its workers, a testament to citizenship rights rather than what the market allows one to buy; the suffragettes, demanding to be equal citizens, citizens of all hues and cries in their post-colonial diversity. In the context of a celebration of "Britishness", these were powerful statements. Becoming a citizen is a continuous struggle of generative resistance that questions the givens of everyday life and that continues to imagine a better civil society and civic options. And, as that other feudal pageant on the Thames suggests, it is a struggle that still has much to overcome: without generative resistance, subjects would be far less citizens and citizens far more subjected.

As a coda, consider the Martin Scorsese film, *No Direction Home,* about the life and times of Bob Dylan, especially the scenes of the young Dylan resisting the labels used by interviewers uninterested in his art and seemingly unaware of its deep roots in American popular cultural idioms. They seek to straight-jacket him, and it is notable that Dylan resists and plays with the interviewers. The resistance provides prep work for one memorable song in particular – "Ballad of a Thin Man" – but this is just one of many lyrics from his youth that expresses a sense of forthright opposition to received wisdom, such as positively 4th Street", with its concluding sneer against those who would resist his resistance: "Yes, I wish that for just one time, You could stand inside my shoes, You'd know what a drag it is, To see you."

TIPS FOR PRACTICE

1. *External peer resistance:* Invite outside experts to a presentation of an idea or a problem you are working on and make them note challenges, contradictory evidence, shaky assumptions, or seemingly illogical reasoning. Let the hottest issues that are identified be the targets of a subsequent collective brainstorm to improve existing ideas or generate new ones.

2. *Internal peer resistance:* Establish rituals and processes for internal challenge and criticism, e.g., by arranging repeated informal give-and-take sessions on work in progress or by playing the role of the devil's advocate for others and encouraging them to do it for you.

3. *Create reviewer roles:* When the size of your practice allows for it, consider having highly qualified, dedicated persons assume formalized roles as reviewers in which they both critique and assist idea work projects. A temporary project-specific review role, such as the Snøhetta groupie scheme, is a less elaborate alternative.

4. *Practice of prolonged conversations:* Cultivate the practice of being in an investigative and explorative mode of thinking, handling large amounts of data and conflicting demands without prematurely reaching for concepts or conclusions.

5. *Maintain tradition but question authority:* Know previous work but be sensitive to its biases, going back to primary inputs (data, client demands) and go through the obdurate facts and assumptions, step by step, that created the solution to those problems.

6. *Challenging with invitation:* Remember that asking "what do you mean?" or "what do you think?" is an invitation to open up. Use opening strategies to express generative resistance – otherwise you may close down the willingness of either the other or yourself to change ideas.

7. *Ask "what if...?" and "how...?"* Repeat.

THINGS TO AVOID

Complacency. Never daring to approach those competitions, tournaments, persons, and rooms that are likely to challenge your idea work at the very edge of your capabilities. Accepting previous work as final and given without questioning it. Attributing non-failure to external authorities rather than working generatively and creatively with them. Shying away from either giving or receiving criticism from others. Taking criticism personally. Not tolerating ambiguity and jumping to conclusions. Embracing a harmony model of creativity and only going for low-risk solutions. Not being able to mobilize sufficient diversity in one's resistance. Believing that resistance is a matter of general techniques independent of domain knowledge.

RESOURCES FOR
LEARNING AND INSPIRATION

Courpasson, D., Clegg, S. R. and Dany, F. (2012). Resisters at work: Generating productive resistance in the workplace. *Organization Science,* 23(3): 801-819. [A study that researches two cases of generative resistance where local management saw and resisted flaws in strategic policy directives from HQ, and were able to use power positively to change strategy.]

Catmull, E. (2008). How Pixar fosters collective creativity. *Harvard Business Review* (September): 64-72. [An article on the many practices of providing generative resistance in the idea work of Pixar.]

de Bono, E. (1992). *Serious Creativity: Using the Power of Lateral Thinking to Create New Ideas.* New York, NY: HarperCollins Publishers, Inc. [One of de Bonos best books, providing techniques for systematically eliciting lateral thinking through challenges, provocations and invertions.]

Dylan, B. (1965). Ballad of a Thin Man, on *Highway 61 Revisited.* New York, NY: Columbia. [Resistance to the stupidity of interlocuters defined and laid out for inspection.]

Dylan, B. (1965/1993) *Positively 4th Street.* New York, NY: Special Rider Music. [Dylan resisting the folk-hero label that had been affixed to his identity – delivered with a winning sneer.]

Locke, K., Golden-Biddle, K. and Feldman, M. (2008). Making doubt generative: Rethinking the role of doubt in the research process. *Organization Science* 19(6): 907-918. [A recent profound article on why embracing resistance by heeding one's doubt can be the primary engine of imagination.]

Nancy, J.-L. (1991). *The Inoperative Community.* Trans. P. Connor et al. (ed.), P. Connor. Minneapolis, MN: University of Minnesota Press. [Being collected by others as a part of a "community" is something to resist, Nancy suggests: community is a dominant Western political formation, founded upon a totalizing, exclusionary myth of unity. More inclusive and fluid forms of being-in-common, of dwelling together in the world, need to be eplored in order to avoid the "iron cage" of community.]

Nemeth, C.J. (2012). Minority influence theory. In Van Lange, P.A.M., Kruglanski, A.W. and Higgins. E. T. (eds.). *Handbook of Theories in Social Psychology.* Vol 2. New York, NY: Sage, pp. 362-378. [A most useful summation of the work of Nemeth and others on the value of dissent in creative processes. Nemeth presents evidence that dissent, even when it is wrong, stimulates divergent thinking, produces more alternatives, and ultimately results in more creative solutions.]

Scorsese, M. (dir.) (2005). *No Direction Home.* Spitfire Pictures. [A documentary film that is interesting for its illustration of the reluctance of the subject and how that reluctance enabled generative resistance to the many identity stereotypes that were attributed to him.]

Stokes, P. (2006). *Creativity from constraints: The Psychology of Breakthrough.* New York, NY: Springer Publishing Company. [A book on how systems of constraints and self-imposed constraints can bolster creativity – rich in examples and largely focused on individuals.]

EXERCISES

1. Why is generative resistance dangerous but necessary?

2. In your kind of work, what do you think represents the lion's cage of generative resistance? What does it take to approach that setting?

3. Is generative resistance necessarily radical or counter-cultural in context?

4. Why might individual ego and pride get in the way of generative resistance?

5. Looking back at your own most successful idea work, how was it resisted in a way that proved generative, and how did you grapple with resistance to it?

6. Think about some of the ways that resistance should be practiced differently in different stages of idea work. How can you best encourage early generative resistance? How would you do this in the last stage of the process?

7. Looking across to other qualities of idea work: In what ways might getting physical enable generative resistance? What is the relation-ship between generative resistance and prepping? Between generative resistance and double rapid prototyping? How, for example, can you involve clients and end users in providing generative resistance?

8. In terms of theories of resistance and power, can you think of contributions that have celebrated resistance per se but that could be reinterpreted in more generative terms?

9. How is resistance related to diversity?

PUNK PRODUCTION

JUST DO IT - YOURSELF!

GUDRUN SKJÆLAAEN RUDNINGEN[1], ARNE CARLSEN,
STEWART CLEGG AND REIDAR GJERSVIK.

Punk pro·duc·tion |
Using audacity and direct, self-initiated action to mobilize
against established ways, opening up and realizing ideas
with high levels of originality and value.

"The most powerful element of the punk project is its underlying refusal to give up on imagining something other than the world as it is... [punks] cannot fully imagine what the better world would look like, but they refuse to accept the one that they know as final."

Stacy Thompson (2004: p. 4). *Punk Productions: Unfinished Business.*

No Elvis, no Beatles,
no Rolling Stones, it's 1977.

The Clash, *1977*

Let's see action, let's see people, let's see
freedom, let's see who cares.

The Who, *Let's See Action*

ANTI AKERSGATA?
"MORE PUNKS PLEASE!"

Kjetil Østli is an award-winning feature journalist, held by many to be the best of his generation in Scandinavia. He looks cool in an unstudied way. Tall, dark, a little reckless and alternative, with his tousled dark hair, his a la mode beard. He talks fast, and he talks well. Many feel they know him through his articles and weekly column in which he writes about his own experiences, often with humor, sometimes self-deprecation, often provocatively, always with a twist. Fewer know that Kjetil rose to his present skill and esteem with a self-confessed punk philosophy of his work. He describes it as:

> "very much an experimental will and a sort of punk attitude against the established folks in Akersgata [a street crowded by major media houses in Oslo]. [...] If you are a bit anti, have this punk attitude, then you are forced to analyze what is not-so-good about the things you are supposed to be anti against."

Kjetil is talking about what made him realize he was a capable writer. The first feature articles from which he received positive feedback had in common that they were all regarded as displaying an experimental form of writing.

> "Those features [the best ones] were always experimental. Like telling a story backwards, like having a quote-driven feature or a line-driven feature, like copying the dramaturgy from movies I liked."

An investigative journalist in the mold of Mikael Blomkvist, of the *Millennium* novels by Stig Larsson, Kjetil writes about provocative issues, often taking unfashionable causes and cases for his material. Paradoxically enough, his credibility is won in precisely that way: being anti-normal, against the stream, pioneering, going his own way. The editors of the weekend magazine where he works not only tolerate this punk attitude, they acknowledge it as an important part of having an independent voice and being a source of new ideas. Thus they encourage it, want to nourish the abnormal and aspire for all of their journalists to break the rules. Is such internalizing and institutionalizing of the function of punk production possible?

WHAT IS PUNK?

Punk has a complex genealogy as a term but is most widely known from its eruption as a music style in the mid-1970s. Everyone knows at least a little bit about what punk music is; think of the Sex Pistols, The Clash, or The Ramones. Anti-authority: short, fast, ragged, music with a do-it-yourself ethos, with no self-indulgence, nothing flatulent or fatuous about it. Hard, driving, exciting music performed by people who were not remote stars but everyday people, close to their audience, at least initially. Striving for advancement, lacking satisfaction of some basic desires, going recklessly into the core of new ideas, all these are significant aspects of punk culture. Punk production rejects "facades of conformity" and opposes false representations of consensus that would bind the punk into dominant authority.

There are two major characteristics that especially apply to punk production in idea work: the concept of being an *outsider within* and the concept of *do it yourself (DIY)*. In punk production, one does not need to be an outsider, but one is deliberately placing oneself on the border by not accepting the dominant order. On the border, a specific outsider sensibility is cultivated, a "site of radical possibility [...] from which to see and create, to imagine alternatives, new worlds" as bell hooks (1990: 149–50) sees it. Opposition is usually associated with threat and therefore punks do not seek to fit in, leaving them an outsider within. Whatever the central value systems might be, punkers will oppose them.

Punk is a "production" that relates to style as much as substance. Its favored mode of action is do-it-yourself. Doing is what is important, often referred to as "direct action". Punks take a provisional attitude toward existing forms of practice. As a creative practice, the "refusal to accept" normalcy can force people to take a stand and explore ideas and practices that lead to radical innovation. Punk production is a temporary break with norms and the dominant order that leads to radical innovations: temporary, because if successful, it creates the new norm.

Punk's success sows the seeds of its own failure. Young punks grow old and punk attitudes, once outside the remit of mainstream society, become a part of the conventional wisdom. Kjetil was initially part of a group of journalists who opposed the establishment in feature writing, in particular as it was expressed in the morning edition of their own newspaper. Today, he will admit, ruefully, that he adjusted to the order after years of being in opposition. But his style is still a little punk.

Don't know what I want, but I know how to get it, I wanna destroy.

Sex Pistols, *Anarchy in the UK*

ANTI-SYSTEM
AND PRO-CUSTOMER

Not only journalists can be punk producers.

Thor Ragnar Klevstuen doesn't look like a punk. He is a little older than Kjetil, for one thing. And he pursues a very different trade, being a successful business developer in a retail bank. Quiet, he displays a faint smile on the surface while, in all probability, reflecting deep beneath. Can such bankers be punk? Well, evidently – Thor Ragnar and his colleagues have repeatedly circumvented the corporate system of idea generation to create and implement their own new ideas, primarily within cash management systems. There are several parallels to the punk production of Kjetil. One is deliberately being an outsider within and keeping integrity in that position:

"The main reason I go to work is that I think it's 'funny shit'. It is important to keep running all the time and not relax. If not, it becomes boring. And also that we in a way – it is perhaps wrong to say – but it is better to ask for forgiveness than permission. Overall we are creating business for our customers. And if we see that we succeed, we ask for money to support the business afterwards instead of beforehand. We do take some chances sometimes."

"I believe the bank will allow us to continue on the same course – if we manage to create something and can demonstrate results. And if we are not allowed to continue, I will quit my job the same day. It's that simple. [...] We are a unit that has achieved much on our own and we've had, in a way, an authorization to maybe go a little outside the specified boundaries. It's really hard to explain, then, but there is something about the feeling of being slightly ahead and spending a lot of time there."

Thor Ragnar and his department maintain their creative deviance by staying under the corporate radar. Another parallel to punk culture is the propensity for speedy direct action, working close to the end users and seeking radically new solutions:

> "Our type of solution is placed in the development of card functionality, even though we are really in the cash management area of the business market. That's what I think makes it a little unique. In other banks the mobile phones are used widely as mobile payment channels. We work with the mobile phone as a payment instrument, so that, for example, I can pay your for lunch by sending you an SMS. On this we work a bit outside the mandate provided by our managers – and that's the way it has to be."

The do it yourself (DIY) attitude often associated with punks is evident in Thor Ragnar's case. DIY presupposes trusting one's instinct, a need to take initiative, and although DIY leans toward individualism in the punk subculture, adherents of this punk ethic can also work collectively. Punk distances itself from commonly accepted norms, supporting anti-established or even anarchist views that seek to free repressed cultural impulses and desires. Punk carries something unexpected and inexperienced with it: It is anomalous. For many organizations this is a threat that should be avoided while for others, probably quite few, it is liberating. Punk production entails danger and threats because it creates a space for new ideas by breaking with norms.

ANTI-TRADITION AND
LOOKING FOR THE BLIND SPOTS

Andreas Helsem does not look much like a punk either. But as an explorer in his mid-thirties, he has a touch of recklessness and audacity about him, with an insistent and direct stare, candid talk, provocative metaphors and use of dramatic pauses – he is someone who demands to be listened to. In mid-2005, Andreas was tired of searching for oil in areas with low prospectivity. He asked for relocation and got one, starting to look at old data in fields with proven oil reservoirs. But it was not until his impatience was recruited into a corporate "Creamed Basin" program that things started to roll. A "creamed basin" represents a basin where the accumulated discoveries form an s-curve (accumulated discoveries on the y-axis, time on the x-axis), with the present being the flat end, much as a surf wave that has curled and creamed: "there is not much left here to find." The rationale for Statoil's Creamed Basin program was a realization that many major discoveries are made in precisely such areas assumed to have creamed but where the models and understanding from existing discoveries or technological limitations – or both – may have worked as blinkers to further search. Thus, a new wave of discoveries based on radical new ideas can seldom be ruled out. In addition, smaller and sometimes faster oil companies were moving aggressively to gain access to areas Statoil had abandoned: what were they seeing?

So when Tim Dodson, chief of exploration in Statoil, asked Andreas in early 2007 to lead one of several Creamed Basin initiatives, he had come to the right man. Andreas's mandate was simply to look for large prospects in mature exploration areas, attacking blind zones and using whatever people and models he wanted. He put together a small team of high-performing explorers (Per Varhaug, Lars Aamodt and Asgeir Bang) with complementary qualities and set out to explore. They were an independent group of radicals, resembling a small firm with the resources of the large organization. The team was shrouded in controversy from the start. Some of their colleagues saw them as self-contained and even arrogant: a group doing their own thing, ignoring other agendas and not spending much time on internal politics to justify their quest.

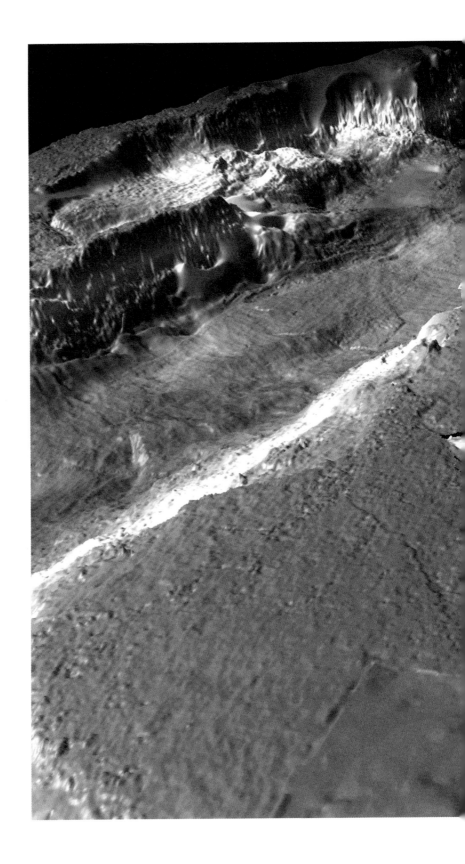

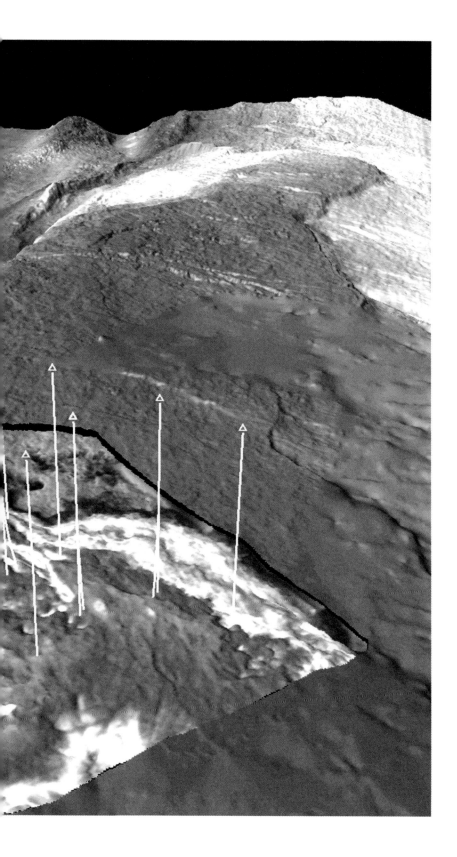

The team thrived. In retrospect Andreas remember it as "just the best time I've had work-wise, the four of us in that room – laughing, quarrelling, working hard, playing loud music, and generating prospects." And there was progress. To make a long story short, Andreas's team made connections between 1) oil shows in the basement rock from an Exxon well in 1967 with 2) a recent spectacular discovery by the small company Lundin (a discovery that, indeed, indicated the importance of the initiative), 3) an argument in a geo-science article from 2006, 4) new shows in the basement rock in a well completed for other purposes, and 5) the discovery of intriguing pressure dynamics. From these new insights, the team came up with a generative question for an area already perforated by wells. Against all previous assumptions, was it possible that there could have been massive deep migration of oil to the east *through* what was known as the Utsira High, an assumed migration barrier? And could there be extractable oil in the supposedly impermeable basement rock?

In the midst of the hard work and heated questioning, the team suggested in the fall of 2007 that another well, one already underway for other purposes, should be extended down to the basement rock to test their theory. The theory was confirmed (though with a different type of oil than the team had suggested), and Andreas could not sleep: "Our first child, a son, had just been born. We had spoiled him with having to be strolled to sleep, and I remember this glorious time of endless walks with the stroller in the streets of Sola at night, completely filled with the futures of both births." As soon as the team had completed their analysis of the key concept, Andreas literally ran up the stairs and stood before the management committee:

"Now you really have to listen well, because what I have to say now will be the most important thing I will ever say in my career as an explorer."

The suggestion was radical: as fast as possible to farm in all available exploration areas near the Utsira high, including areas recently abandoned. The management committee moved on the suggestion instantly. Not all theories were proven right, for as Andreas said: "We were right about everything in general and wrong about many of the particulars." But the speed paid off. The project ended up in a discovery at present estimated (by independent news services) to be between 1.7 and 3.5 billion barrels of high quality oil, literally in the company's backyard – one of the largest discoveries ever on the Norwegian shelf.

Andreas, being the team leader, was allowed to suggest the name for the prospect. He chose "Aldous" from his favourite author, Aldous Huxley. Huxley, a rebel for his time, and in many ways a punk, had written about "doors of perception", which later inspired the name of the iconic rock band The Doors. With the discovery, the hit "Break On Through to the Other Side" took on a new meaning for Andreas. After the discovery became a fact and was charged with economic and political significance, the more conservative name of Sverdrup (after Johan Sverdrup, a well-known politician and statesman) resulted. The team – the explorer punk band – had more ideas in other areas, radical ideas. But priorities had now shifted and the band split up.

> *You know that day destroys the night, night divides the day. Tried to run, tried to hide, break on through to the other side.*

The Doors, *Break On Through*

The learning point from all of this is not that all exploration should be punk-oriented, or that punk-like attitudes are a guarantee of success. To begin with, punk explorers must have deep knowledge of the tradition they oppose. The punk-dimension of the Aldous/Sverdrup discovery was more anti-tradition than anti-organization, a resistance to established ways of thinking and to the rigidities of assumptions that may stop new ideas from emerging. In this respect the team was typically punk: it was fuelled by radical autonomy; it had strong anti-sentiments; it bucked the basis of previous success; it represented a bet on the future in search of past glory but using different instruments and interpretations this time round.

Generally, the quality of punk production is fundamental as a never-ending source for revitalizing one's idea work. Kjetil Trædal Thorsen, Chief Architect at Snøhetta and responsible for many groundbreaking and award-winning architectural designs worldwide, recognizes:

> "No, that (perfection) does not exist. Well, the moment I have *that* feeling I have nothing more to do. So I hope that I'll never feel that it is perfect. Well, the meaning in all this is, I hope, that we manage to radicalize even more than we are now. I feel that as a result of becoming more mature as an organization, we should have the ability to become more and more radical instead of more conformist because we can challenge more powerful authorities in society. The stronger you are, the stronger your position to challenge the existent."

In this regard, even business lawyers have their punk side. Borgar Høgetveit Berg tells us that, for a lawyer, the will to challenge the established law may sometimes be what makes the difference:

> "Sometimes it is important to have self-confidence and say: 'I don't give a damn about what Gjeldsvik wrote in 1936, he was wrong!' But there are a lot of people who don't do that. You can call it creativity, but it is for the most part about the professional knowledge and the ability to challenge the written words – the ability and the will to challenge."

Few people in organizations are punks all the time. But all of us can think of examples where we have participated in something resembling punk production. Therein lies the liberating prerogative. It need not be a big revolution or involve buying into a lifestyle of purple hair and uncomfortable needles in strange places. Punk is essentially about seizing the moment and just doing it – yourself!

ANTI-SELF AND
CHOOSING A PUNK ALIAS

Bob Dylan, after being over-produced on many of his records, (especially Daniel Lanois's production of *Oh Mercy*, where he is swamped on some tracks in echo) increasingly took over the production himself in his later years under the pseudonym of "Jack Frost". Dylan is famous for resisting too much in terms of rehearsal or multiple attempts at recording a song. If it can't be nailed in one or two takes, it probably won't be nailed at all on that occasion. Perfection is unimportant – what counts is getting the feeling right. He is also famous for hardly ever sticking to the arrangements on his records during live concerts. Once the architecture of a song is in place, it can be performed in many ways, he says. A performance becomes an occasion to challenge one's self, one's band, and one's audience – the true punk ethos that shines through the great live version of "Idiot Wind" recorded in driving rain on the album *Hard Rain*, about which one fan, Craig Paul, writing on Amazon, says "The studio track dripped blood. This live rant just splatters it all over the place. The beauty of the song is that Dylan's voice and phrasing are just so perfectly annoying that they take this hymn of hate way over the top, right where it should be. When Bob gnarls "I kiss goodbye the howling beast on the borderline which separated you from me," it makes "It Ain't Me, Babe" sound like "You Light Up My Life" with Debbie Boone. Exactly: punk production pushes, provokes, and protests against predictability.

When you got nothing,
you got nothing to lose.

Bob Dylan, *Like A Rolling Stone*

TIPS FOR PRACTICE

1. *Just Do-It-Yourself!* DIY is about seeking knowledge oneself regardless of previous efforts, position, or resources. The most basic action mantra of punk production is thus: whatever the system says, whatever lack of resources or fear of reprimand, when an opportunity for developing and realizing radical ideas emerges, *seize* it, *act* on it, don't wait for resources, don't wait for permission, do it *now*, do it yourself!

2. *Define something you are against*: Punk production gains fuel by being against something, whether internal or external to the organization. Try to define it. It might be an irritating industry convention, a non-discussable taken-for-granted topic or a once-celebrated practice that has now paled and become rigid. It might even be the organization's crown jewels. What annoys, irritates, or seems old and/or unnecessary? Attack it.

3. *Experiment with breaking norms*, sometimes just for the sake of it, to see what happens. The risk is social rejection and being recognized as a threat because one fails to fit in. Who cares – at least *new* things happen. The experience one gains from taking care of the matter oneself opens up new possibilities. Reduce large problems to a manageable size. Start with small experiments that lead to bigger "packages" of change. Pick battles carefully.

4. *Give people freedom*: Punk production requires space, thrives on autonomy, and loves challenges that come without prescriptions on how to meet them. Trust employees with time to work on topics they have chosen on their own and symbolically reward them for success in doing so. Introduce slacker awards, punk awards, do the famous Skunk works, but, however you do this, allow people autonomy. No successful punk band was ever established and controlled by the establishment.

5. *Act authentically and spontaneously*: Express your own beliefs, feelings, and identities directly to create resistance to authorities and
   to minimize feelings of self-doubt, fraudulence, or guilt. Don't be a
   punk "poseur" who pretends to be something that he's not. DIY.

6. *Keep affiliations and sidetracks*: Maintain strong ties and spend
   time with radical individuals, communities, and groups outside
   your organization for sources of information, resources, emotional
   support, and empathy. Invite radical outsiders to attend internal
   meetings.

7. *Jujitsu language*: Use the rhetoric of your opponent or those in power
   to get your ideas across.

THINGS TO AVOID

Sticking to routines. Stressing the traditions of the organization. Waiting
for permission or resources. Underestimating the space one's leaders
are willing to provide for radical initiative. Expecting someone else to
do your punk work for you. Being suspicious of outsiders and challenges
from within. Strong founders who grow old and their ideas stale with
them. Letting the punk attitude go in times of fear – when there is an
economic downturn or recession. Not daring to be radical enough:
The cutting edge should cut.

RESOURCES FOR
LEARNING AND INSPIRATION

Dylan, B. (1976). "Idiot Wind", from *Hard Rain*. New York, NY: CBS Records. [Punk!]

Carter, L., Ulrich, D., and Coldsmith, M. (2005). *Best Practices in Leadership Development and Organization Change.* Chapter 11: Mattel. San Francisco, CA: Pfeiffer, pp. 263–280. [A documentation of the Platypus project at Mattel, the largest toymaker in the world. Platypus is the name for a re-occurring 12 week product development process that is self-organized and may be seen as an attempt at institutionalizing punk-like mecha-nisms for idea work. See also http://www.businessweek.com/stories/2005-07-18/project-platypus-reinventing-product-development-at-mattel.]

Godin, S. (2011). *Poke the Box: When Was the Last Time You Did Something for the First Time?* USA: Do You Zoom, Inc. [A series of amusing and stimulating paragraphs and one-liners that testifies to the value of direct non-conforming action.]

books, b. (1990). *Yearning: Race, Gender, and Cultural Politics.* Boston, MA: South End Press. [bell hooks is and American author, feminist, and social activist and a punk-style writer. Her real name is Gloria Jean Watkins, taking her pen name bell hooks (intentionally uncapitalized) from her great grandmother. This is a collec-tion of essays in which hooks rails against a broad range of topics on gender, race, teaching, and the significance of media for contemporary culture.]

Laing, D. (1985). *One Chord Wonders: Power and Meaning in Punk Rock.* Milton Keynes and Philadelphia: Open University Press. [A celebration of the DIY ethos of punk.]

Mainemelis, C. (2010). Stealing fire: Creative deviance in the evolution of new ideas. *Academy of Management Review* 35(4): 558–578. [A theoretical paper that bridges creativity and deviance literature to propose a theory of a nonconforming behavior that is not inherently positive or negative, but that involves stealing time to produce creative outputs.]

Meyerson, D. (2003). *Tempered Radicals. How People Use Difference to Inspire Change at Work.* Boston, MA: Harvard Business School Press. [A wonderful treatise on how organizations can be the home to and even stimulate radicals that are given free reign but are also tempered for organizational ends.]

http://punkademics.com/blog [Can academ-ics also be punks? A blog trying to explore the seemingly contrary worlds of punk and academia. There is a book of the same name that features original essays, interviews, and selected reprints on the boundaries between punk culture, politics, and higher education.]

Rudningen, G. (2011). Punk production. Enacting radical innovation by breaking norms in organisational idea work. Paper presented at the 27th EGOS colloquium in Gøteborg, July 6–9. [A precursor to parts of this chapter.]

Thompson, S. (2004). *Punk Productions: Unfinished Business.* New York, NY: State University of New York Press. [A concise history of punk music from the perspective of a materialist theory of punk economics and aesthetics committed to transform-ing consumers into producers. The author voices opposition to globalization, includ-ing objectification of subjectivity through consumption of ready-made things.]

EXERCISES

1. How could organizations nourish the nonconformity of punk production?

2. Can you think of examples of punk production in organizations you have worked in, or in your work as a student?

3. Punk production celebrates just doing it, rather than making it perfect: How can clients and customers be engaged in this? Is there a role for punk in prototyping?

4. Should organizations that want to change kick out the jams made by strategists and planners and engage with punks instead? Could these modes of exploring the future co-exist?

5. If you were to liberate your inner punk self, freeing it from repression, what would you do differently? Why? What is the most punkish thing you have ever done?

6. How does punk production relate to generative resistance? What are the pitfalls to being punk *and* being generative?

7. Must punk be anti-authority?

8. Must punk production always be self-initiated?

PAGE	PLACEMENT	INSTITUTION	PHOTOGRAPHER
13	All except 2nd row left	iStock	Not available
13	2nd row left	Idea work	Aina Landsverk Hagen
Introduction			
17	Middle	Idea work	Aina Landsverk Hagen
20	Middle left	Snøhetta	Snøhetta
20	Bottom right	Snøhetta	Christopher Hagelund
20	Bottom left	Snøhetta	Snøhetta
20	Middle right	Snøhetta	Snøhetta
24	Bottom	Idea work	Tord F. Mortensen
25	Top right	Idea work	Gudrun Skjælaaen Rudningen
25	Middle right	Snøhetta	Siri Warren
25	Bottom right	Snøhetta	Aina Landsverk Hagen
25	Middle left	Snøhetta	Siri Warren
29	Bottom	Aftenposten/ NTB scanpix	Jan Thomas Espedal
Prepping			
47	Bottom	Snøhetta	Siri Warren
49	4 pictures	Snøhetta	Siri Warren
52	Bottom	iStock	Not available
53	Bottom	Statoil	Ian Sharp
Zooming out			
66	Middle	Statoil	Statoil
69	Bottom	iStock	Not available
72–73	Middle	Snøhetta	Snøhetta, sketches by Squared design lab
Craving wonder			
89	Bottom	Snøhetta	Siri Warren
92–93	4 pictures	Snøhetta	Snøhetta, sketches by Squared design lab
94	Bottom	iStock	Not available
Activating drama			
105	4 pictures	Snøhetta	Gerald Zugmann
106	Bottom	iStock	Not available
109	Top	Idea work	Tord F. Mortensen
109	Bottom	iStock	Not available
Daring to imagine			
122	2 pictures	Snøhetta	Åke Lindmann
124	Bottom	Aftenposten/ NTB scanpix	Jan Thomas Espedal
126	Middle	Statoil/WesternGeco	Audun Groth
Getting physical			
142	Top	Idea work	Arne Carlsen
142	Middle	Statoil	Statoil
142	Bottom	University of Technology, Sydney	Not available
146	Bottom	Idea work	Aina Landsverk Hagen
147	Top	Aftenposten/ NTB scanpix	Jan Thomas Espedal

148	Top left	Idea work	Tord F. Mortensen
148	Top right	Snøhetta	Siri Warren
148	Middle right	Idea work	Gudrun Skjælaaen Rudningen
148	Middle left	Snøhetta	Siri Warren
148	Bottom	Idea work	Tord F. Mortensen
149	Top left	Snøhetta	Siri Warren
149	Top right	Snøhetta	Siri Warren
149	Middle left	Snøhetta	Siri Warren
149	Middle right	Snøhetta	Siri Warren
149	Bottom	Idea work	Tord F. Mortensen
152	Bottom	Idea work	Aina Landsverk Hagen
154	2 pictures	Idea work	Gudrun Skjælaaen Rudningen

Double rapid prototyping

162	Bottom left	Snøhetta	Siri Warren
162	Middle left	Aftenposten/ NTB scanpix	Jan Thomas Espedal
162	Middle right	Snøhetta	Aina Landsverk Hagen
162	Top right	Idea work	Aina Landsverk Hagen
163	Top left	Idea work	Arne Carlsen
163	Middle left	Idea work	Gudrun Skjælaaen Rudningen
163	Top right	Idea work	Gudrun Skjælaaen Rudningen
163	Top/middle right	Idea work	Gudrun Skjælaaen Rudningen
163	Middle right	Idea work	Gudrun Skjælaaen Rudningen
166	Bottom	Snøhetta	Siri Warren
167	Middle	Snøhetta	Siri Warren
170–171	Middle right	Idea work	Aina Landsverk Hagen
172–173	Middle left	Snøhetta	Christopher Hagelund

Liberating laughter

183	Bottom	Snøhetta	Trond Fjørtoft
186	Middle	Idea work	Gudrun Skjælaaen Rudningen
186	Bottom	Idea work	Arne Carlsen
187	Bottom	Idea work	Tord F. Mortensen
188	Top	Snøhetta	Siri Warren
188	Bottom left	Idea work	Tord F. Mortensen
188	Bottom right	Idea work	Gudrun Skjælaaen Rudningen

Generative resistance

199	Bottom	Snøhetta	Snøhetta
201	Middle	Snøhetta	Marianne Sætre
201	Left	Snøhetta	Bartek Milewski
201	Right	Snøhetta	Snøhetta, sketches by White view
203	Bottom	Snøhetta	Snøhetta, sketches by White view
205	Middle right	Idea work	Gudrun Skjælaaen Rudningen
205	Bottom	Idea work	Gudrun Skjælaaen Rudningen
205	Middle left	Aftenposten/ NTB scanpix	Jan Thomas Espedal
206	Top	Idea work	Gudrun Skjælaaen Rudningen
206	Middle	Snøhetta	Siri Warren

Punk

217	Top	iStock	Not available
224–225	Full	Statoil	Statoil

ENDORSEMENTS

"Prepare to be surprised. This book on idea work significantly enriches how we see, understand and do the everyday work of making ideas transformative. The book is simultaneously simple and profound, playful and serious, practical and theoretical. No doubt it will be useful and used by anyone who is curious about how ideas become real in everyday activities. The book makes the process of idea work accessible and mysterious at the same time. No matter what your interest is in idea work, read a page, read a chapter, read the whole book – any engagement with the book will excite novel thought and practical advice – a rare and pleasing combination."

Jane Dutton, Robert L. Kahn Distinguished University Professor of Business Administration and Psychology, University of Michigan

"This book is an explosive package of insight, cutting edge methodology, ready-to-implement instruments and elevating inspiration. Exciting to glance and compelling to read systematically, the book walks its talk. It is perhaps the most uplifting and yet realistic book on organizational innovation and creativity I know. Deeply embracing the seemingly mundane actions of practitioners in a number of different fields, the book is an empirically informed synthetic conceptualization of positively deviant organizational creativity. While scholarly impressive and highly useful as a guide to the frontiers of the research, the book entirely avoids the pitfalls of overtheorizing. The book sets your ideas in motion - and in ways that will take you by surprise. The book "activates the drama" of your internal angels of creativity, inspires your "craving wonder", will encourage you "to zoom out" and look with "daring imagination" for possibilities of "punk production". Idea work starts to emerge - in the reader of *Idea Work*."

Esa Saarinen, Professor of Applied Philosophy at the School of Science, Aalto University

"It is a rare book that celebrates the life, passion, and wonder of ideas at work. It is a rare book that is as at home with professionals who long for sound practical advice about how to work with ideas more effectively, as it is with business scholars who long for sound theoretical abstractions to explain such work more sensitively and completely. It is a rare book about creativity that is itself creative in its form and style; that marries the vibrant nuances of real world stories with the incisive and compelling concepts of social science theory at its best. And it is a rare book that leaves readers – practitioner and academic alike – with the happy and even grateful sense of understanding a little bit more of the inexhaustible mystery of the human mind at work. This is that rare book."

Lloyd Sandelands, Professor of Management and Organizations & Professor of Psychology, University of Michigan

"Great idea! The decision to examine the world of ideas and ideas at work was a great, well, idea. This is where it all starts. Management scholars have been recently obsessed with knowledge management, execution, competitive advantage and design. But before these processes enter the scene all that there is an idea. With its sophisticated and distinctive Nordic touch, this book is not only mandatory read for those interested in the power of idea work, but also a beautiful object of design. A pleasure to the eye and to the mind."

Professor Miguel P. Cunha, Universidade Nova de Lisboa

"Innovation makes life duller in many organizations across the globe these days. A wonderful idea has transformed into a dominant management discourse, which stifles creativity and new ideas wherever it goes. It is for this particular reason that I was glad to read *Idea Work*. Rather than a managerial pamphlet promoting another way for the top management to control their firms, it is a book about how real people work in search of new ideas. I envy the authenticity the authors reach in the case illustrations and enjoy the insights within the text. This book should be read by those interested in where ideas come from in organizations."

Professor Saku Mantere, Head of Department, Management and Organization, Hanken School of Economics and Business Administration

"The growing interest for practice based studies has found its way to creativity and innovation studies in this beautifully designed book *Idea Work*. Carlsen, Clegg and Gjersvik take an almost anthropological view on daily activities of those involved in idea creation in organizations. The empirical rich book provides the reader new, detailed and applicable understandings of how people in organizations engage, create, materialize, communicate, resist and realize ideas. Research on creativity and innovation has never been so 'down to earth' and inspire us to see creativity through a practice lens. The found qualities of idea work are valuable to academics, students and practitioners in the field of creativity, innovation and design."

Professor Alfons van Marrewijk. Professor in Business Anthropology, VU University Amsterdam

"Reading this book enables us to appreciate that extraordinary idea work lies essentially in performing ordinary activities, in a whole range of work settings, extraordinarily - with love. *Idea Work* captures not just the dynamic processes that make the impossible possible. It arrests the magic of doing what we do for the love of it, and what it has the potential to create. A must read for anyone who cares to live a more fulfilling (working) life!"

Elena Antonacopoulou, Professor of Organizational Behaviour at University of Liverpool Management School/Senior Fellow of Aim (the Advanced Institute of Management Research)

"In a world where ideas matter, where they come from, how they are generated and under what conditions they grow and ripen are important questions. This remarkable book does not have any single answer to these questions but many, because it is in the nature of 'idea work' that it can be structured and serendipitous, individualistic and collaborative, inspiring and banal. Yet the authors recognise that there is also a common thread in such work – it requires courage and the capacity for free and critical thinking to tackle the 'tyranny' of the blank page, not just the page that's already written. This is also the value of the book for business educators. We need to spend as much time on the rewards of taking risks as on the techniques and costs of managing them."

Professor Roy Green, Dean, UTS Business School, University of Technology Sydney

"How refreshing to see a book that lives up to its word and succeeds in illuminating serious play in a seriously playful manner. A delight to read!"

Professor Richard J. Badham, Macquarie Graduate School of Management

"By exploring idea work in practice, *Idea Work* drafts a picture of innovation and creativity in the context of everyday work that very topically departs from perspectives centered on heroic narratives or project management techniques. It will offer a strong basis for further research as well as inspiration and reflection for practice."

Professor Emmanuel Josserand, CMOS, University of Technology, Sydney